HARCOURT

Science

Harcourt School Publishers

Orlando • Boston • Dallas • Chicago • San Diego

www.harcourtschool.com

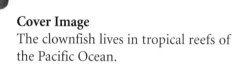

Cover Image
The clownfish lives in tropical reefs of the Pacific Ocean.

Printed in the United States of America

ISBN 0-15-317496-X

4 5 6 7 8 9 10   032   2002   2001

Authors

Marjorie Slavick Frank
Former Adjunct Faculty Member at
    Hunter, Brooklyn, and Manhattan
    Colleges
New York, New York

Robert M. Jones
Professor of Education
University of Houston-Clear Lake
Houston, Texas

Gerald H. Krockover
Professor of Earth and Atmospheric
    Science Education
School Mathematics and Science
    Center
Purdue University
West Lafayette, Indiana

Mozell P. Lang
Science Education Consultant
Michigan Department of Education
Lansing, Michigan

Joyce C. McLeod
Visiting Professor
Rollins College
Winter Park, Florida

Carol J. Valenta
Vice President—Education, Exhibits,
    and Programs
St. Louis Science Center
St. Louis, Missouri

Barry A. Van Deman
Science Program Director
Arlington, Virginia

UNIT A

Life Science

Plants and Animals All Around

Life Science

Living Together

Earth Science

About Our Earth

UNIT D

Earth Science

Weather and the Seasons

UNIT E

Physical Science

Matter and Energy

UNIT F

Physical Science

Energy and Forces

Using Science Skills

Observe

Compare

Sequence

8 days   22 days   35 days

Classify

Infer

Gather Information

Plan

Make Models

Measure

Predict

Draw Conclusions

How Many Paper Clips?

0 1 2 3 4

Communicate

Science Safety

Think ahead.

Be neat.

Be careful.

Do not eat or drink things.

Safety Symbols

CAUTION Be careful!

CAUTION Sharp!

CAUTION Be careful!

CAUTION Wear an apron.

CAUTION Wear goggles.

Plants and Animals All Around

Life Science

Plants and Animals All Around

UNIT PROJECT

Watch Me Grow!

Plan a class aquarium. Find out what things plants and animals need to live there.

1

Living and Nonliving Things

senses

living

nonliving

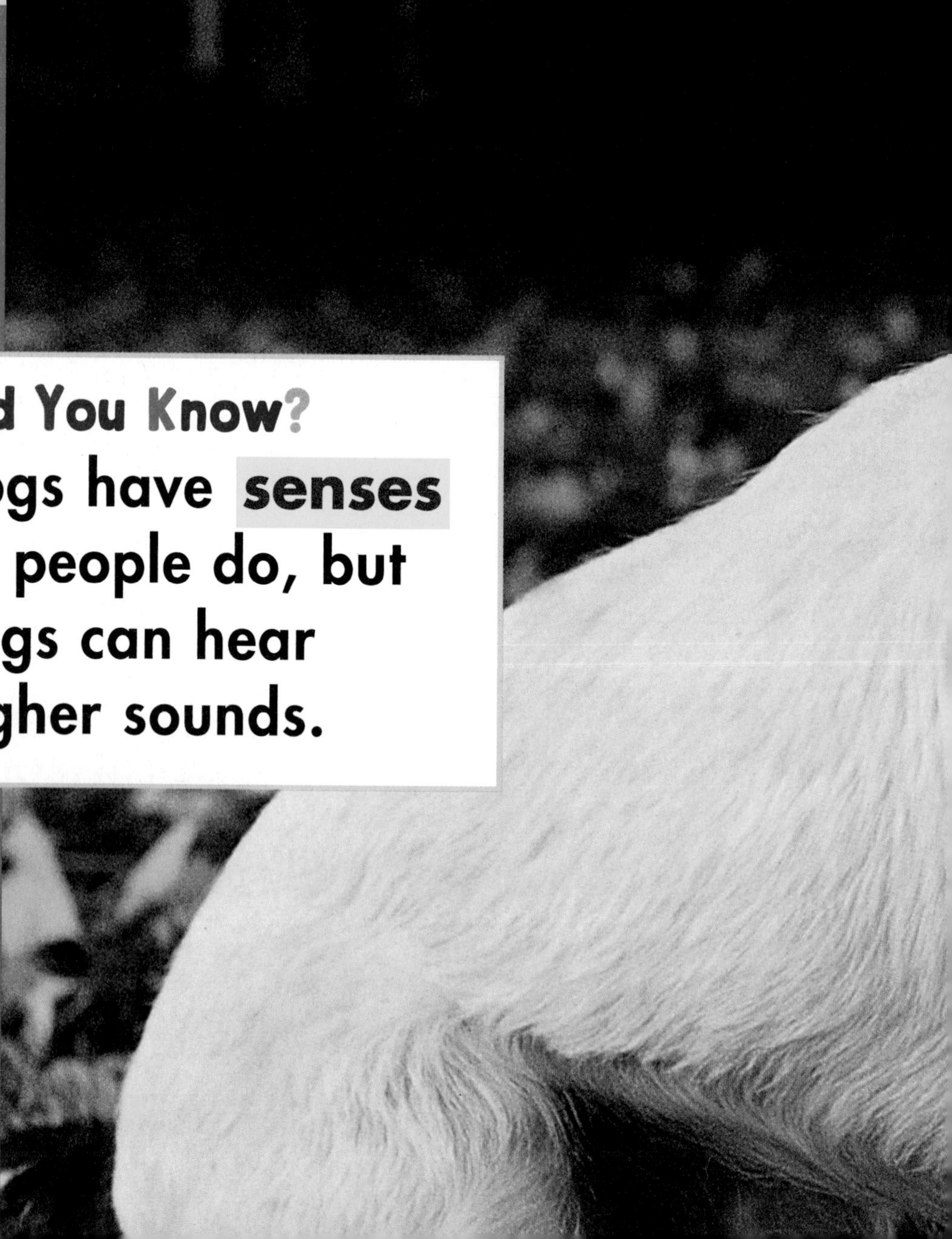

Did You Know?
Dogs have senses
as people do, but
dogs can hear
higher sounds.

Did You Know?

The oldest **living** thing on Earth is the bristlecone pine tree in the United States.

How Do My Senses Help Me Learn?

Using Your Senses

You will need

pieces of fruit

plastic gloves

1 Close your eyes. Your partner will put on gloves and give you a piece of fruit.

2 Touch and smell the fruit. Tell what you observe. Name the fruit.

3 Take turns with your partner.

Science Skill
When you observe things, use more than your eyes to find out about them.

Your Five Senses

You have five **senses** that help you learn about things. What part of your body do you use for each sense?

sight

smell

touch

hearing

taste

Sight

Your sense of sight helps you learn
how things look.

■ **What can the boy learn
by looking at the fish?**

Touch

Your sense of touch helps
you learn how things feel.

- **What can the girl
  learn by touching
  the kitten?**

Hearing

Your sense of hearing helps you learn about sounds.

■ **What sound does this boy hear?**

Smell

Your sense of smell helps you learn how things smell.

■ **How do you think these flowers smell?**

Taste

Your sense of taste helps you choose what to eat.

■ **How do you think these grapes taste?**

Think About It

1. What are the five senses?

2. How do your senses help you learn?

What Are Living and Nonliving Things?

Investigate

A Mealworm and a Rock

You will need

mealworm

rock

 hand lens

 bran meal

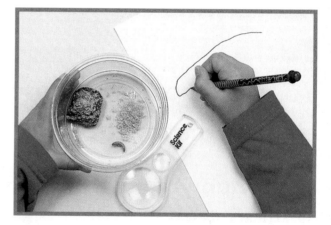

1 Give bran meal to the mealworm and the rock. Use the hand lens to observe.

2 Does the mealworm or the rock move or eat? Draw what you see.

3 Compare the mealworm and the rock. Which is a living thing?

Science Skill

When you compare things, you tell how they are the same and different.

Living and Nonliving Things

Plants, animals, and people are **living** things. They need food, water, and air to live and grow. **Nonliving** things do not need food, water, and air.

nonliving

living

Living Things

Flowers and dogs are living things. They need food, water, and air to grow and change. They come from other living things.

■ **How do you know the flower is a living thing?**

Nonliving Things

A rock and a chair are nonliving things.
They do not need food, water, and air.
They do not grow.

■ **How can you tell these are nonliving things?**

Compare Living and Nonliving Things

How can you tell if something is living?
Ask these questions.

- Does it need food, water, and air?
- Does it grow and change?

If you say yes both times, the thing is living.

■ How are these bears the same?

■ How are they different?

These pictures show living things and nonliving things. Water can move, but it is a nonliving thing. It does not need food and air.

■ **Which things in these pictures are living and nonliving?**

Think About It

1. What is a living thing?
2. What is a nonliving thing?

Health/Career Link

A Doctor Observes People

This doctor is using her senses as she gives the boy a checkup. She listens to his heart. She looks at his throat.

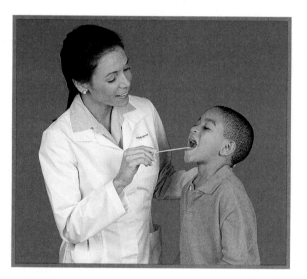

■ **Which sense is the doctor using in each picture?**

Think and Do

Draw a picture of a doctor. Then show your picture. Tell how doctors use their senses in their work.

Measure with a Growth Chart

This girl can tell she is growing. Her mother measures her on a growth chart. She is taller now than she was a year ago.

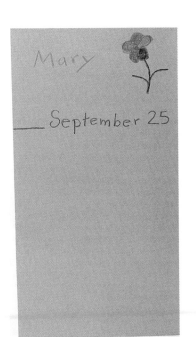

Mary

September 25

Think and Do

Make a growth chart. Have someone help you mark how tall you are. Write the date. Measure how tall you are each month.

Tell What You Know

1. Which senses would you use to learn more about each thing?

Vocabulary

Tell which pictures go with the words.

2. living thing

3. nonliving thing

a.   b.   c.   d.

Using Science Skills

4. Observe Collect things in an egg carton. Use two words to tell how each thing feels, looks, sounds, or smells. Have a partner guess each thing.

5. Compare Make a chart to compare a pencil and a plant. Draw pictures of them. Tell if the things are living or nonliving.

Living or Nonliving?			
Thing	Picture	Does it need air and water?	Does it grow?
pencil			
plant			

CHAPTER 2

All About Plants

Vocabulary

roots

stem

leaves

flower

seed

seed coat

sunlight

Did You Know?
The rafflesia is the biggest flower in the world.

Did You Know?
There is a plant that has leaves that look like elephant ears.

What Are the Parts of a Plant?

Plant Parts

You will need

carrot

plant with flower

paper and pencil

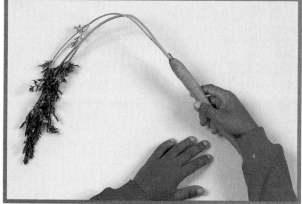

1 Look at the parts of one plant. Draw what you see.

2 Look at the parts of the other plant. Draw what you see.

3 Compare the plants. Tell about their parts.

Science Skill

When you compare things, you tell how they are the same and different.

Parts of a Plant

Plants have different parts. Most plants have roots, a stem, and leaves. Many plants also have flowers.

flower

leaf

stem

roots

How Plant Parts Help a Plant

Plants have many shapes and sizes.
Most plants have the same parts.
These parts help them live and grow.

Roots

The **roots** hold plants in the soil. The roots also take in water.

■ **What part of a carrot do you eat?**

■ **Where are the stems in these pictures?**

Stems

The **stem** helps hold up the plant. Water moves up the stem to the leaves.

A tree trunk is also a stem. Water moves up the trunk to the tree's leaves.

Leaves

The **leaves** make food for the plant. Leaves from different plants have different shapes.

■ **What shapes do you see?**

Flowers

Many plants also have flowers.
The **flowers** make seeds.

■ What part of the plant is this bee on?

Think About It

1. How are plants the same?
2. How are they different?

How Do Plants Grow?

Investigate

The Inside of a Seed

You will need

bean seed

hand lens

1 Peel off the covering of the seed.

2 Open the seed.

3 Observe. Tell what is inside.

Science Skill

Use a hand lens to help you observe.

How Plants Grow

Most plants grow from a **seed**. The seed may have a covering called a **seed coat**. The seed coat falls away as the plant grows.

leaves

stem

seed

seed coat

roots

A29

Plants Grow from Seeds

Different plants grow from different seeds. The new plants look like the plants the seeds came from. When old plants die, their seeds can be planted to grow new plants.

■ **Observe the seeds. How are they the same and different?**

tomato seeds

sunflower seeds

apple seeds

corn seeds

dandelion seeds

orange seeds

Think About It

1. Where do new plants come from?
2. What will the plant that grows from a seed look like?

What Do Plants Need?

What Plants Need to Grow

You will need

seeds

2 clear cups

any color cup

soil

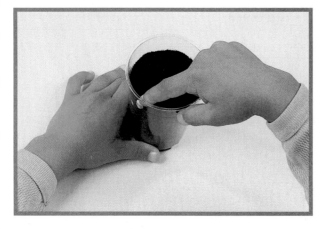

1 Fill one clear cup with soil. Plant two seeds near the side. Water.

2 Put the cup with the seeds into the cup with color. After 3 days, take it out.

3 Share what you see.

Science Skill

When you share your ideas, you **communicate** with others.

What Plants Need to Live

Plants need four things to live and grow.
What are these four things?

air

light

soil

water

How Plants Grow and Live

Light and Air

A plant's leaves use light and air to make the plant's food. Light from the sun is called **sunlight**.

Water

Plants also need water to grow and stay healthy. Water helps move food to all parts of the plant.

■ How do this plant's leaves help the plant live?

Different kinds of plants grow in different places around the world. All these plants need light, air, and water.

■ **Where is the water in each of these pictures?**

Think About It

1. What do plants need to live and grow?

2. How do leaves use light and air?

Art Link

An Artist Observes Plants

An artist named Vincent van Gogh painted these flowers long ago. Artists look closely at things around them.

Sunflowers by Vincent van Gogh

■ **What parts of a plant can you see in this picture?**

■ **What part is missing?**

 **Think and Do**

Paint your own picture of a plant. Show at least two parts.

Measure a Plant

You can use a ruler to measure how tall a plant grows. You can also use a pencil or a stick if you do not have a ruler.

Think and Do

Watch a plant grow. Put a pencil in the soil next to the plant. Mark how tall the plant is. Every three days, mark how much the plant has grown.

Tell What You Know

1. Tell what you know about each picture.

Vocabulary

Tell which picture goes with each word
or words.

2. roots

3. leaves

4. stem

5. flowers

6. sunlight

7. seed

8. seed coat

a.   b.   c.   d.

e.   f.   g.

Using Science Skills

9. Compare Roots take in water. Stems help plants stand up. Think about the parts of your body that take in water or help you stand up. How are you the same as a plant? How are you different?

10. Observe Make a chart about leaves where you live.

Find two leaves. Glue or tape them on your chart. Tell about your leaves.

Leaves			
Leaf	Shape	Color	Size

All About Animals

Vocabulary

gills

mammal

reptile

amphibian

insect

hatch

larva

pupa

tadpoles

Did You Know?
A gecko is a
reptile that can
crawl up trees.

Did You Know?

There are more kinds of beetles than any other kind of **insect**.

What Do Animals Need?

An Animal Home

You will need

plastic box and gloves

soil, twig, and rocks

water in a bottle cap

small animals

1 Put the soil, twig, rocks, water, and animals in the box.

2 Observe. How does your home give the animals food, water, and a place to hide?

3 Draw what you see. Close the lid.

Science Skill

When you observe the animals in their home, you can see how they meet their needs.

What Animals Need

All animals need food, water, air, and a place to live. These ducks live by a pond. Why is this a good home for them?

mallard ducks

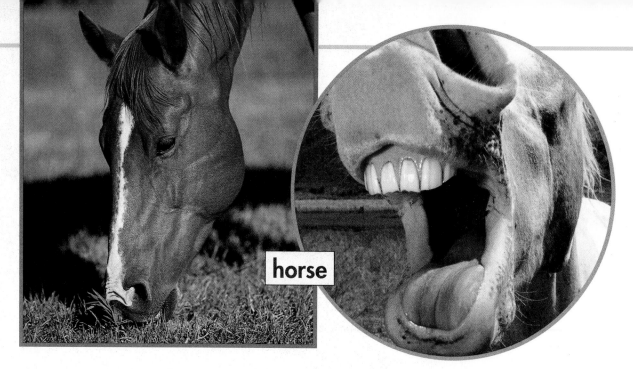

horse

Animals Need Food

Different kinds of animals need different kinds of food to live and grow. Horses eat grass, but lions eat meat. A horse's flat teeth are good for chewing grass. A lion's sharp teeth are good for tearing meat.

■ **What do an animal's teeth tell you about what it eats?**

mountain lion

Animals Need Water

All animals need water to live. Like many animals, a camel drinks with its mouth. It also gets water from the food it eats. An elephant uses its trunk to put water in its mouth.

■ **How are the camels and the elephant getting the water they need?**

camels

elephant

Animals Need a Place To Live

All animals need a place to live.
A bat can find a home in a cave.
A falcon can build a nest.
Animals keep safe and raise their
young in their homes.

bat

peregrine falcons

Park Ranger

Many animals have homes
in parks. If they need help,
park rangers take care of
them.

Animals Need Air

All animals need air to live and grow. Special body parts help them get it. Some animals have a nose and lungs. Others, like this fish, have **gills** that take air from water.

cow

gills

Think About It

1. What do animals need to live and grow?
2. What are some ways animals meet these needs?

What Are Some Kinds of Animals?

Investigate

Animals in Your Neighborhood

You will need

paper and pencil

1 Observe different kinds of animals in your schoolyard.

2 Draw a picture of each animal you observe.

3 Classify the animals into groups. How are the animals in each group the same?

Science Skill

When you classify animals, you observe how they are the same. Then you group them.

Different Kinds of Animals

reptile

Scientists observe how animals are the same and different. They put animals that are the same into groups. Here are some kinds of animals.

birds

fish

mammal

amphibian

Mammals

A **mammal** is an animal that feeds its young milk. A mammal also has hair or fur on its body.

- How can you tell these animals are mammals?

whitetail deer

pig

squirrel

Birds

Birds are animals that have two wings and two feet. They are the only animals that have feathers. Some birds fly, some birds run, and some swim.

macaw

bluebird

flamingo

■ How are all these birds the same?

Reptiles

A **reptile** is an animal with rough, dry skin. It may have scales or hard plates. Alligators and turtles are reptiles.

alligators

giant tortoise

Amphibians

An **amphibian** is an animal with smooth, wet skin. Frogs, toads, and salamanders are amphibians.

salamander

■ How are amphibians different from reptiles?

Fish

Fish live in water. They have special body parts called gills that help them breathe. Their bodies are covered with scales.

snapper

gills

queen angelfish

■ How are these fish the same?

Think About It

1. What are some different kinds of animals?

2. How are the animals in all the groups the same? How are they different?

What Are Insects?

A Model of an Insect

You will need

Styrofoam balls   scissors   toothpicks and chenille sticks   wax paper

1 Choose an insect to make. Insects have three body parts and six legs.

2 Choose materials. Make a model of your insect.

CAUTION Be careful with toothpicks, chenille sticks, and scissors. They are sharp.

3 Compare your model with a picture of a real insect.

Science Skill

When you make a model of an insect, you show parts that a real insect has.

A54

Insects

An **insect** is an animal that has three body parts and six legs. Some insects also have wings.

3 body parts

weevil

More About Insects

Insects lay eggs. A ladybug lays hundreds of eggs at one time.

Insects do not have bones. They have a strong body covering. The covering keeps their soft insides safe.

ladybug

■ **What else do you think the body covering does for the grasshopper?**

grasshopper

A butterfly is an insect. It uses its wings to fly. An ant is an insect, too. Most ants have no wings. They use their legs to move fast.

■ **How are the butterfly and the ant the same and different?**

butterfly

ant

Think About It

1. How can you tell if an animal is an insect?
2. What else do you know about insects?

How Do Animals Grow?

Animals and Their Young

You will need

animal picture cards

paper and pencil

Animals and Their Young		
Animal	Same	Different
cats	Both have ears. Both are orange.	One is big. One is small.

1 Match the picture cards. Put each young animal with the adult.

2 Make a chart. Compare the young animal and the adult.

3 Tell how each young animal is like the adult. Tell how it is different.

Science Skill

When you compare the pictures, you tell how they are the same and different.

How Different Kinds of Animals Grow

These young animals will change as they get older. They will grow to look like their parents.

 bunny

 chick

Ways Animals Begin Life

Rabbits are small when they are born. Their eyes are closed. They can not walk or hop until they are older.

just born

8 days old

■ **How do the chick and the rabbit change in different ways?**

Chicks **hatch**, or break out of eggs. Their eyes are open. Soon they can walk and peck for food.

just hatched

8 days old

8 weeks old

adult

8 weeks old

adult

Animals Care for Their Young

Some animals feed their young. Later they teach them how to find food.

robins

brown bears

■ **How do these animals make sure their young have food?**

Some animals lick their young to clean them. Later they show them how to clean themselves.

chimpanzees

Some animals stay close to their young to keep them warm. Others keep their young warm in pouches.

■ **How do these penguins keep their baby warm?**

emperor penguins

Think About It

1. What are two ways that animals begin life?
2. How do all young animals change as they grow?

How Does a Butterfly Grow?

A Butterfly's Life

You will need

box

caterpillar

paper and pencil

1 Keep your caterpillar in a warm place.

2 Observe your caterpillar every day for three weeks. Draw it each time.

3 How did your caterpillar change? Share what happened.

Science Skill

When you use your senses to observe, you find out how the caterpillar changes.

How a Butterfly Grows

A butterfly is an insect. It hatches from an egg. It changes many times before it grows colorful wings. What do all insects have?

monarch butterfly

From Caterpillar to Butterfly

A butterfly begins life as an egg. A tiny caterpillar, or **larva**, hatches from the egg. The caterpillar eats and grows.

1 egg

2 caterpillar or larva

3
pupa

4
butterfly
comes out

Then it stops eating. The caterpillar becomes a **pupa** and makes a hard covering.

Inside the covering, the pupa slowly changes. Finally a butterfly comes out and flies away.

 5 adult butterfly

Wings Help Butterflies Keep Safe

Butterfly wings have different shapes and colors. Some wings look like leaves or flowers. These wings help butterflies hide.

Buckeye

Spring Azure

Tiger Swallowtail

Other wings help butterflies trick hungry birds.

■ **How do you think "eye spots" might trick a bird?**

Owl

Dogface

Think About It

1. How does a caterpillar change into a butterfly?
2. What are some ways wings help butterflies keep safe?

How Does a Frog Grow?

A Frog's Life

You will need

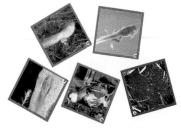

picture cards

1 Put the picture cards in sequence. Show how you think a frog changes as it grows.

2 Tell why you put your cards in the order you did.

Science Skill

When you sequence the cards, you show what happens first, next, and last.

How a Frog Grows

A frog is an amphibian. It hatches from an egg. As it grows, it changes many times. When it is an adult, it has long back legs.

leopard frog

From Tadpole to Frog

Frogs lay their eggs in water. Young frogs, or **tadpoles**, hatch from the eggs. They have tails to move and gills to breathe in water. They grow.

■ **How has this tadpole changed?**

3 tadpole with back legs

2 tadpole

1 frog eggs

The tadpoles keep changing. They grow front legs. They get lungs to breathe air. Their tails get smaller. Then they look like little frogs. They climb onto land and grow bigger.

4

tadpole grows front legs, tail gets smaller

Think About It

1. How does a tadpole change into a frog?
2. What body parts does a tadpole have that a frog does not have?

5 adult frog

Movement/Drama Link

Move Like a Frog

These children think about a time in a frog's life. Then they move to show what that time is like.

Think and Do

Find an open space on the floor. Show what a frog does as an egg, a tadpole, or an adult frog.

Find Symmetry

Look at this butterfly's wings. Find the two parts that match. Use your finger to trace a line between the matching parts.

Think and Do

Make a butterfly with wings that match.

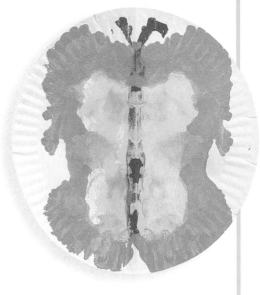

Fold a paper plate in half. Open the plate, and paint patterns on one half. While the paint is wet, press the two halves together. Then open the plate.

How are the two parts the same?

Tell What You Know

1. Tell how these animals are the same.
Then tell how they are different.

Vocabulary

Tell which picture goes
with each word.

2. mammal

3. reptile

4. amphibian

5. insect

6. gills

7. pupa

8. tadpole

9. hatch

10. larva

a. **b.** **c.**

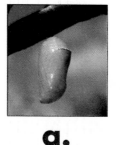

d. **e.** **f.**

g. **h.** **i.**

Using Science Skills

11. Classify Make a graph to show groups of animals. Find pictures of animals. Classify your pictures to make a graph like this one.

Insects | Amphibians | Mammals | Fish | Reptiles | Birds

12. Sequence A butterfly changes as it grows. Write the words in sequence to show how this insect changes.

adult butterfly

larva

egg

pupa

Senses Game

Get a box and put in different things. Ask your family or classmates to close their eyes. Have them use touch and hearing to guess each thing.

Nature Walk

Take a nature walk with your class or with family members. Draw or write about what you observe.

Growing and Changing

Look at photos of yourself with a family member. Talk about how you have changed.

Observe a Pet

With an adult, find a pet to observe. Draw or write about the animal.

What does the pet look like?

What does it eat and drink?

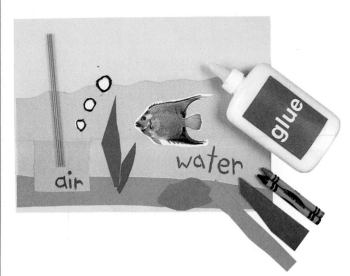

WRITING

Collage What do plants or pets in a classroom need to live? Make a picture. Write your ideas.

READING

The Very Hungry Caterpillar **by Eric Carle** How does the hungry caterpillar use plants? Share your ideas.

 COMPUTER CENTER Visit *The Learning Site* at www.harcourtschool.com

Living Together

Life Science

Living Together

UNIT PROJECT

Take a Peek!
Find out how plants and animals live in different places. Decorate a box that shows one place.

CHAPTER 1

Plants and Animals Need One Another

Did You Know?
Some animals such as the clownfish use other animals for shelter.

Did You Know?
Ragweed **pollen** has sharp points that make people sneeze.

How Do Animals Need Plants?

Investigate

How Small Animals Use Plants

You will need

timer or watch   string loop   paper and pencil

1 Go outside with your class. Observe animals and plants inside your string loop.

2 Observe and record for five minutes. How are animals using plants?

3 Share what you observed.

Science Skill

As you observe, use your senses of sight, hearing, and smell to help you.

How Animals Need Plants

Many animals need plants for food.
Some animals use plants to hide in or to
make nests for their young.

rabbit

carrot top

Animals Need Plants for Food

Some animals eat only plants. Rabbits eat the tops and the roots of carrot plants. Caterpillars eat leaves.

■ **What does this cow eat?**

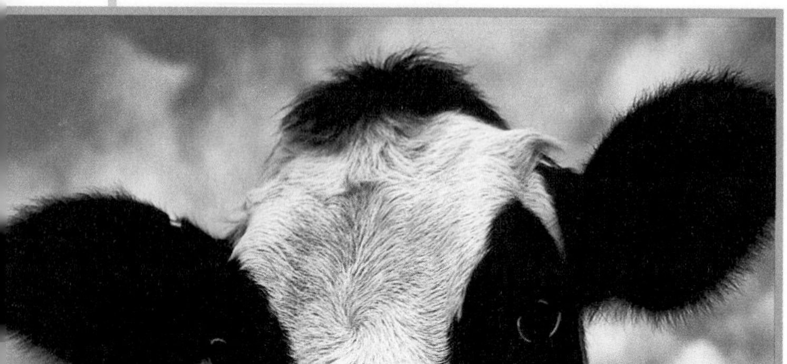

cow

caterpillar

Some animals eat other animals as well as plants. A toucan eats insects as well as fruit. A raccoon eats both fish and berries.

■ **What is this raccoon eating?**

raccoon

toucan

Other Ways Animals Need Plants

Some animals need plants for shelter. A **shelter** is a place where an animal can be safe.

African leopard

■ How does the tree help this leopard keep safe?

termites

Many animals that live in the soil need plants for shelter. They may live inside rotting logs. They eat bits of dead plants.

Some animals make nests with parts of plants. A bird may use grass. An alligator uses leaves and strong reeds.

oriole

alligator

deer mice

■ **What do mice use to make a nest?**

Think About It

1. What are some ways animals need plants?
2. What animals eat only plants? What animals eat other animals as well as plants?

How Do Animals Help Plants?

How Seeds Stick to Animals

You will need

Styrofoam ball

glue

cotton and other materials to try out

1 Look at this picture. How might these seeds stick to animals?

2 Plan a model of a seed that sticks. Choose materials to glue to the ball.

3 Investigate your materials. Which ones stick to the cotton? The cotton is like animal fur.

Science Skill

To investigate how seeds stick to animals, make a plan to try out different ideas. Follow your plan.

How Animals Help Plants

Some animals carry seeds to new places. Some help make the soil better for plants. Others help flowers make seeds.

Animals Carry Seeds

A seed may stick to a cat's fur. The seed may be carried far from the plant. When the seed falls off, it may grow into a new plant.

seed bur

Animals Help Make Soil Better

earthworm

A worm eats dead plants. Its waste helps **enrich** the soil, or make the soil better for plants.

■ What things are these animals doing that help plants?

Animals Help Plants Make Seeds

Flowers have a powder called **pollen** that helps them make seeds. A butterfly carries pollen from flower to flower. The pollen falls off. Those flowers use the pollen to make seeds.

butterfly

Think About It

1. How do small animals make the soil better for plants?
2. How do animals help plants grow new plants?

How Do We Need Plants and Animals?

Things People Use

You will need

picture cards

1 Which pictures show things made from plants? Which are from animals?

2 Classify the cards. Sort them into groups.

3 Share your groups. Tell why each thing belongs.

Science Skill

When you classify the things on the cards, you group them to show ways they are the same.

How People Need Plants and Animals

People need plants and animals for food, clothing, and shelter. Plants and animals also add beauty to people's lives.

What People Need Plants For

People need shelter and clothing. They use plants to make many products. A **product** is something that people make from other things.

cotton shirt

cotton bolls

■ **Where did the lumber come from to make this house?**

People eat parts of plants.
Celery is the stem of a
plant. Peanut butter is
made from peanuts,
the seeds of a plant.

■ **What plant do
you like to eat?**

People also use
plants to make
products they need
in their homes.

What People Need Animals For

People use animals for food. Many people eat beef, pork, chicken, and fish. Eggs and milk are also foods from animals.

■ **What parts of this breakfast come from animals? What parts come from plants?**

People use wool from sheep to make clothing. Coats and sweaters may be made with wool.

Guide Dog Trainer

Some people keep animals as pets. Others need animals as helpers. Guide dog trainers work with some dogs. They teach them to help blind people.

Think About It

1. What are some ways people need plants?
2. What are some ways people need animals?

Math Link

Snacks Made from Plants

People make snacks from plants. They mix nuts, dried fruits, and cereal to make a tasty treat. Stores may call this snack *trail mix*.

Think and Do

Make a snack from plants. Measure one cup each of granola, raisins, and nuts into a bowl. Mix them. Eat your trail mix snack.

Keeping a Custom

Long ago, some African Americans in South Carolina made baskets like this one. They wove them from plants. This woman keeps the custom. She weaves a basket as people did long ago.

Think and Do

Paper comes from plants. It is made from the wood of trees. Use strips of colored paper to weave a place mat.

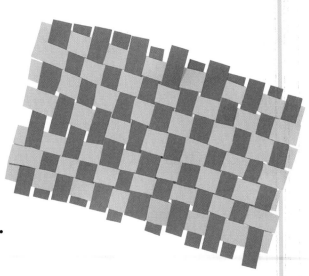

Tell What You Know

1. Tell how animals and people can use these plants to meet their needs.

Vocabulary

Tell which picture goes with each word. Then use the word to tell about the picture.

2. enrich

3. shelter

4. pollen

5. product

a.   **b.**

c.   **d.**

Using Science Skills

6. Classify Collect pictures of different kinds of foods. Put the foods that come from plants in one group. Put the foods that come from animals in another group.

What foods can you find that come from both plants and animals?

7. Observe Make a chart about the ways you use plants and animals. Observe ways you use them at school. Draw pictures in your chart.

Ways I Use Plants and Animals			
	Food	Clothing	Beauty
Plants			
Animals			

A Place to Live

Vocabulary

forest
desert
rain forest
ocean
algae

Did You Know?
Squirrels in the **desert** use their tails like beach umbrellas to stay cool.

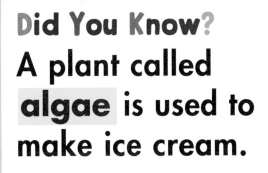

Did You Know?
A plant called
algae is used to
make ice cream.

What Lives in a Forest?

Forest Trees

You will need

dark crayon

pencil and paper

1 Go outside. Find a tree. Draw one of its leaves.

2 Make a rubbing of the tree's bark.

3 Compare your drawing and rubbing with a classmate's.

Science Skill
When you compare drawings and rubbings, look for ways the trees are the same and different.

Forests

A **forest** is a place where many trees grow. A forest floor is shady. The soil stays moist.

forest

Forest Plants and Animals

Some trees grow tall in a forest. Their high leaves catch the sunlight they need to make food.

Berry bushes and mountain laurels need less sunlight than trees. They can grow below the trees.

berry bushes

mountain laurel

Many animals find food and shelter in a forest. Wood thrushes find safe places to build their nests. Box turtles eat worms for food.

wood thrushes

red foxes

■ How are the foxes meeting their needs?

box turtle

Think About It

1. What is a forest?
2. How do plants and animals in a forest meet their needs?

What Lives in the Desert?

Desert Leaves

You will need

2 paper clips

water

wax paper

2 paper-towel leaf shapes

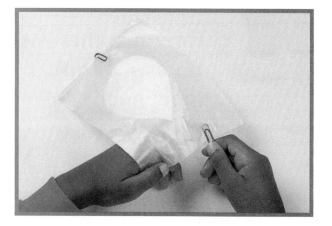

1 Make both leaf shapes damp. Put one shape on wax paper. Fold the paper over. Clip it.

2 Put both leaves in the sunlight. Check them after an hour.

3 Which leaf holds water longer? Draw a conclusion.

Science Skill

To draw a conclusion about desert leaves, think about your leaf with the waxy coat and the other leaf.

Deserts

A **desert** is a dry place. It gets lots of sunlight and little rain. Only a few kinds of plants and animals can live there.

desert

Desert Plants and Animals

Desert plants can hold water to use when they need it. Some, like the yucca, have thick leaves with a waxy coat. Others hold water in their thick stems.

cactus wren

yucca

beavertail cactus

Most deserts are hot. Desert animals have ways to stay cool and get water. Some, like the armadillo, stay in the shade. They look for food at night when it is cooler. Others, like the kangaroo rat, get water from their food.

■ **How do many of these animals stay cool?**

armadillo

rattlesnake

kangaroo rat

Think About It

1. What is a desert?
2. How do plants and animals live in a desert?

What Lives in a Rain Forest?

Rain Forest Plants

You will need

seeds

2 wet cotton balls

film cans and lid with hole

plastic and rubber band

wet cotton ball

seeds

wet cotton ball

seeds

plastic

rubber band

1 Rain forest plants get little light. Make a model of a rain forest like this one. Close lid.

2 Plants in open areas get more light. Make a model of an open area.

3 Set both models in the sun for 5 days. Tell how the cotton changes.

Science Skill

To **communicate** how the forests grew, draw and share pictures of what you observed.

Rain Forests

A **rain forest** is wet all year. Most rain forests are warm, too. Rain and warm weather help trees and other plants grow. Animals use the plants to meet their needs.

rain forest

Rain Forest Animals and Plants

Animals live at different levels of the rain forest. Macaws live near the treetops. They find fruit to eat. Sloths hang from the middle of trees. They find shelter there and plants to eat.

macaw

three-toed sloths

orchid

Rain forest plants also live at different levels. Most grow from roots in the soil. Some, like the orchid, grow from roots halfway up trees. They get the light they need there.

bromeliad

Think About It

1. What is a rain forest?
2. How do plants and animals live in a rain forest?

■ Where does the rain forest plant called a bromeliad live?

What Lives in the Ocean?

Ocean Animals

You will need

ocean picture cards

1 Which ocean pictures show fish? Which show other animals?

2 Classify the animals. Put them in groups.

3 Share your groups. Talk about other ways to classify the animals.

Science Skill

When you classify the animals, you group them to show ways they are the same.

Learn About

Oceans

An **ocean** is a large, deep body of salt water. Oceans cover three fourths of the Earth.

ocean

Ocean Plants and Animals

Some ocean plants are called **algae**. Many ocean animals use algae for food and shelter.

parrot fish

■ **What is the parrot fish using the algae for?**

bottle-nosed dolphin

green sea turtle

starfish

Ocean animals can find what they need in ocean waters. Dolphins' strong tails help them swim fast to catch fish.

Sea turtles use their flippers to swim and catch food.

■ **How do you think a starfish's shape helps it get food?**

Think About It

1. What is an ocean?
2. How do ocean animals get what they need to live?

Math Link

Observe Leaf Patterns

You can find leaf patterns on a tree twig. A tree grows leaves the same way again and again. The leaves make a pattern.

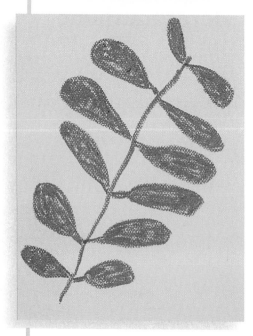

Think and Do

Look at a tree twig with leaves. Observe how the leaves grow in a pattern. Draw a picture that shows the pattern.

A Scientist Investigates the Ocean

Sylvia Earle is a marine biologist, a scientist who studies life in the ocean. She dives deep to find out about ocean plants and animals. She also helps people learn about the ocean.

Think and Do

Choose a plant or an animal that lives in the ocean. Read books to learn more about it. Make a poster that tells about the plant or animal.

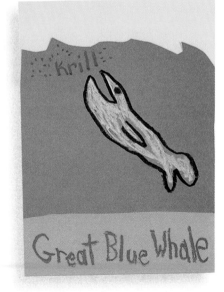

Krill

Great Blue Whale

Tell What You Know

1. Tell about where each animal lives.

Vocabulary

Tell which picture goes with the
word or words.

2. algae

3. rain forest

4. ocean

5. desert

6. forest

a.   b.   c.

d.   e.

Using Science Skills

7. Classify Read the clues. Name each plant or animal. Tell where it lives.

a. This plant has thorns that keep animals from eating it. It has a waxy coat to keep water in.

b. This animal has fins for swimming. It uses algae for food and shelter.

c. This plant lives halfway up on trees. It needs a warm, wet place.

8. Compare Look at the graph. Tell which place gets the most rain in a month.

How Much Rain Falls in a Month?	
Temperate Forest	⬇ ⬇ ⬇ ⬇ ⬇
Rain Forest	⬇ ⬇ ⬇ ⬇ ⬇ ⬇ ⬇ ⬇ ⬇ ⬇ ⬇ ⬇ ⬇ ⬇ ⬇
Desert	⬇

Each ⬇ equals 2 centimeters.

What Do Worms Need?

1. Put two kinds of soil and two worms in a covered box.

2. In two hours, check where the worms are.

3. What do the worms need? Talk about what you observe.

Make a Bird Feeder

1. Spread peanut butter on a pinecone.

2. Roll the pinecone in birdseed.

3. Hang the pinecone with string outdoors.

4. Observe birds that eat the seeds.

Rain Forest in a Jar

1. Put pebbles, soil, and plants in a jar.

2. Water the plants. Put the lid on the jar.

3. Put the jar where it gets light but not strong sun.

4. Wait one day. Observe. How is this like a rain forest?

Stems That Store Water

1. Observe the stem pipes, or small dots on a cut celery stalk.

2. Set the stalk in an empty cup. Put it in the sun until it droops.

3. Add water to the cup. Put it in the refrigerator. The next day, tell what happened and why.

stem pipes

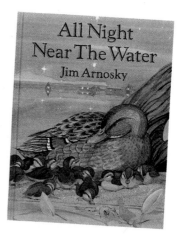

WRITING

Pop-Up Card Fold a sheet of paper. On the outside, write a question about a place. Inside, give a pop-up answer!

READING

All Night Near the Water
by Jim Arnosky
How do ducks and other animals use a lake for shelter and food? Talk about what you find out.

COMPUTER CENTER
Visit *The Learning Site* at
www.harcourtschool.com

About Our Earth

UNIT
C

Earth Science

About Our Earth

UNIT PROJECT

On Land and Sea
Make a mural. Show land, air, water, and how people use these things.

Earth's Land

Vocabulary

sand
rock
soil
texture

Did You Know?
Centipedes have
up to 100 pairs of
legs that help them
grip the **soil**.

Did You Know?
Chalk is **rock** made from the bones of tiny sea animals.

What Can We Observe About Rocks?

Ways to Classify Rocks

You will need

hand lens

different rocks

paper and pencil

Rocks			
Red			

1 Observe each rock with the hand lens. Feel each rock. Write how the rocks look and feel.

2 Make a chart. Classify your rocks on the chart.

Science Skill

When you classify your rocks, you group them by ways they are the same.

Rocks

A **rock** is a hard, nonliving thing that comes from the Earth. There are many kinds of rocks. People use rocks in different ways.

Different Kinds of Rocks

Some rocks are big, and some are small. Tiny broken pieces of rock are called **sand**. Rocks may be different colors. Some rocks are smooth. Others are rough.

sand

rose quartzite

lava

marble

obsidian

limestone

■ How are these rocks the same? How are they different?

People use rocks to build homes
and walls. They melt sand to
make glass.

■ **How have these
people used
rocks?**

Think About It

1. What are rocks?

2. What ways do people use rocks?

What Is Soil?

Observing Soil

You will need

soil

paper plate

hand lens

paper and pencil

Soil		
Looks	Smells	Feels

1 Make a chart like this one. Then observe the soil with a hand lens. Move the soil around.

2 Smell and feel the soil. Think of words that tell about it.

3 Draw pictures and write words that tell about the soil.

Science Skill

When you observe the soil, use your senses to find out how it looks, smells, and feels.

Soil

The Earth's **soil** is made of tiny rocks. It has bits of dead plants and animals in it. Soil has air and water in it too.

All Living Things Use Soil

Plants need soil to grow. Soil has water that plants need. Small pieces of dead plants and animals in soil enrich it.

soybeans

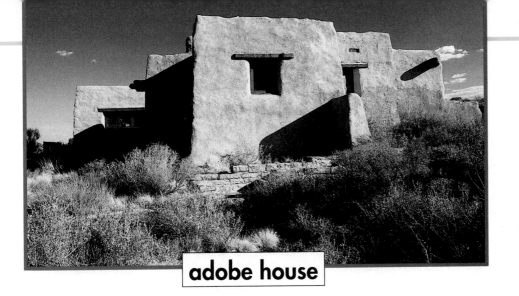

adobe house

People use soil in different ways. Farmers use soil for growing foods. Builders mix soil, water, and straw to make bricks.

Some worms and insects live in soil. Many other animals use soil to make shelters.

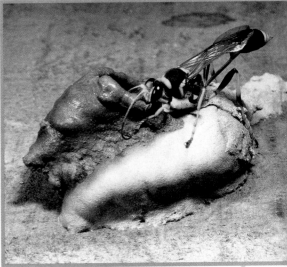

■ How do you think this insect uses soil?

Think About It

1. What is soil made of?
2. What are some ways plants and animals use soil?

C11

How Do Different Soils Compare?

How Soils Compare

You will need

hand lens

3 kinds of soil

paper plate

spoon

1 Observe each kind of soil. How does it smell and feel?

2 Put some of each soil on the plate. Use the hand lens to observe.

3 Compare the three kinds of soil. Tell your classmates about them.

Science Skill

When you compare the soils, you tell how they are the same and different.

Different Soils

There are different soils. Each has a different mix of rocks and plants and animal bits. The **texture** of the soil is how it feels.

topsoil

clay soil

sandy soil

How Soils Are Different

Topsoil is dark brown. It has many bits of dead plants and animals in it. Topsoil clumps when it is squeezed. It can hold water.

topsoil

Clay soil may be yellow, red, or brown. It feels sticky, and it clumps when it is squeezed. Clay soil can hold a lot of water.

clay soil

Sandy soil is often light brown. The sand in it makes it feel rough. It does not clump much when it is squeezed. It also does not hold water well.

sandy soil

Think About It

1. What are some different kinds of soil?
2. What are some ways soils are different?

A Geologist Observes Rocks

Florence Bascom was the first American woman to become a geologist. A geologist is a person who studies rocks.

In summer Florence Bascom collected rocks. In winter she studied and wrote about them.

Think and Do

Collect some rocks. Read books to find out about them. Then make a display that tells others what you learned.

Measure Mass

Long ago, people used rocks to measure mass. They put an object on one side of a balance. They added rocks to the other side until the two sides balanced. The number of rocks told the mass of the object.

Your baby weighs 2 stones.

Think and Do

Collect some rocks that are about the same size. Use a balance to measure the mass of some objects.

Tell What You Know

1. Look at the pictures. Tell what you know about each kind of soil.

Vocabulary

Tell which picture goes with each word.

2. sand

3. rock

4. soil

5. texture

a. **b.**

c. **d.**

Using Science Skills

6. **Classify** Find two kinds of soil where you live. Put each kind in a small bag. Then make a chart like this one. Tape the bags to your chart. Label each bag *topsoil, clay soil,* or *sandy soil.*

Kinds of Soil Where I Live			
Kind of Soil	Color	How It Feels	How It Smells
topsoil			
clay soil			

7. **Compare** Scientists compare how hard rocks are. You can, too. Find different rocks. Use a nail to scratch each one. Soft rocks scratch easily. The hardest rocks won't scratch at all.

Which rock is the hardest? Which is the softest? Tell how you know.

Earth's Air and Water

Vocabulary

air
fresh water
stream
river
lake
salt water

Did You Know?
The largest **lake** in the world is in North America.

Did You Know?
You can move **air** from one container to another underwater.

Where Is Air on Earth?

Air in a Bag

You will need

plastic bag

1 Pull an open bag toward you. Then hold the top of the bag closed.

2 Squeeze the bag. What do you observe? Poke a hole in the bag.

3 What was in the bag? How did you infer that?

Science Skill

When you infer, you use what you observe and know to make a good guess.

Where Air Is

Air is something that people can not see, taste, or smell. Yet air is all around.

■ **What is lifting up the kite in this picture?**

Air Is All Around

You can not see air, but you can see what it does. Air can blow the leaves of trees.

You can feel air when it blows on your skin. You can feel air move through your nose and into your body.

■ How do you know air is in these pictures?

Air is in the soil under your feet. It is also in the water you drink.

Air is in the streams, rivers, lakes, and oceans of the Earth. Most of the plants and animals of the Earth need air to live.

Think About It

1. How do you know where air is?

2. Where is air?

Where Is Fresh Water Found?

Investigate

Making Salt Water Fresh

You will need

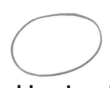

rubber band

salt, bucket, and sand

marbles and plastic wrap

2 cups and water

1 Mix some salt in water. Taste the water. Pour the water into the bucket. Throw away used cups.

2 Put another cup in the bottom of the bucket. Cover. Put marbles on top.

3 Place the bucket in the sun. Wait two hours. Take the cup out. Taste the water. Draw a conclusion.

Science Skill

To draw a conclusion, think about what you observed and what you know about water.

Fresh Water

Water that is not salty is called
fresh water. Rain is fresh
water. Rain makes puddles or
sinks into the ground.

Where Fresh Water Comes From

Rain and melted snow run down mountains. They may form a **stream**, a small body of moving water.

The stream may flow into a **river**, a larger body of moving water. The river flows into a lake. A **lake** is a body of water with land all around it.

stream

river

lake

People need fresh water for drinking, cooking, and washing.

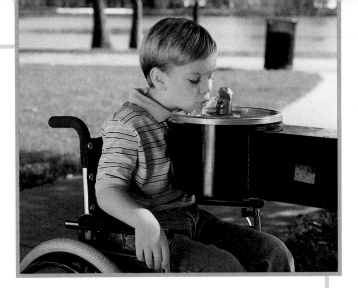

Water Testers

Water from lakes and rivers is cleaned. Then people can drink it. A water tester checks water. The clean water flows through pipes to people's homes.

Think About It

1. What is fresh water?
2. Where do we find fresh water?

Where Is Salt Water on Earth?

Investigate

Salt and Salt Water

You will need

hand lens   salt and spoon   cup of water   plate

1 Observe salt on a plate. Draw or write about it.

2 Stir the salt into the water until you can not see it. Write about it.

3 Put some salt water on the plate. Leave it all night. Then communicate what is left on the plate.

Science Skill

When you communicate, use your writing to help you tell others what you observed.

Salt Water

Water that has salt in it is called **salt water**. Salt water tastes and smells salty. The water in the oceans is salt water.

Where Salt Water Is

Salt water is in oceans which cover most of the Earth. Salt water is also in some rivers that flow into oceans. A few lakes have salt water, too.

■ **What part of the Earth looks blue from space?**

How Salt Water Is Used

In some places, people take the salt out of ocean water. Then they have fresh water to use. They may use the salt on their food.

Think About It

1. What is salt water?
2. Where is the Earth's salt water?

The Puddle
by David McPhail

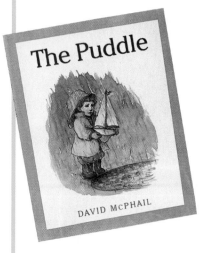

In this book, a boy starts to sail his boat in a puddle. Then some animal friends come by and everything changes.

Have someone share *The Puddle* with you. Find out how the boy and his friends use the puddle. See what happens when the sun comes out.

Think and Do

Make a puddle on a plastic plate. Use a crayon to draw around it. Let the sun shine on your puddle. Observe what happens.

Math Link

How Much of the Earth Is Ocean?

Oceans cover most of the Earth. In fact, oceans cover three fourths of it.

Think and Do

Use a paper plate to show how much of the Earth oceans cover.

1. Fold a paper plate in half.

2. Fold the plate in half again the other way. You will have four parts called fourths.

3. Color three of the fourths blue.

4. Color one fourth brown.

Tell What You Know

1. Tell what you know about each picture.

Vocabulary

Tell which picture goes with the word or words.

2. air

3. fresh water

4. stream

5. river

6. lake

7. salt water

a.   **b.**   **c.**

d.   **e.**   **f.**

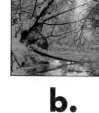

Using Science Skills

8. **Infer** Hold a cup upside down. Push it under the water. Then tip it to one side. Observe. Infer what was in the cup.

9. **Communicate** Get a cup of fresh water and a cup of salt water. Put a few drops of each kind on ice. What happens?

Make a chart. Tell how fresh water is different from salt water. Communicate to classmates what you find out.

Fresh Water and Salt Water Are Different		
	Fresh Water	Salt Water
How Does It Look?		
How Does It Taste?		
What Does It Do to Ice?		

Observe Soil Layers

1. Put soil in a jar.
2. Fill the jar with water.
3. Put the lid on tight. Shake.
4. Wait for the soil to settle. Draw what you observe.

Make a Soil Key

1. Fold an index card into four parts. Cut a hole in the middle.
2. Color each part black, brown, yellow-orange, or orange-brown.
3. Put the card on top of some soil near your home. Which color matches?
4. Brown and black soils are good for growing plants. Tell about your soil.

How Much Air Is In a Breath?

1. Take a big breath.

2. Let it out by blowing into a balloon.

3. With your fingers, hold the end of the balloon closed. Observe how much air you breathed out.

4. Compare balloon breaths to a classmate's or family member's.

Visit a Shoreline

1. With your class or family members, visit a shoreline.

2. Observe the soil. Dig at it.

3. Draw pictures of any shells, rocks, plants, or animals you observe.

4. Share your drawings.

WRITING

Earth Book Make a book in the shape of Earth. On each page, tell one way people use air, water, rocks, or soil.

READING

Water
by Frank Asch
Where is water on Earth? How is it used? Read and share your ideas.

COMPUTER CENTER
Visit *The Learning Site* at
www.harcourtschool.com

Weather and
the Seasons

UNIT D

Earth Science

Weather and the Seasons

UNIT PROJECT

The Four Seasons
Make a mobile for each season. Show plants, animals, weather, and clothing.

CHAPTER 1

Measuring Weather

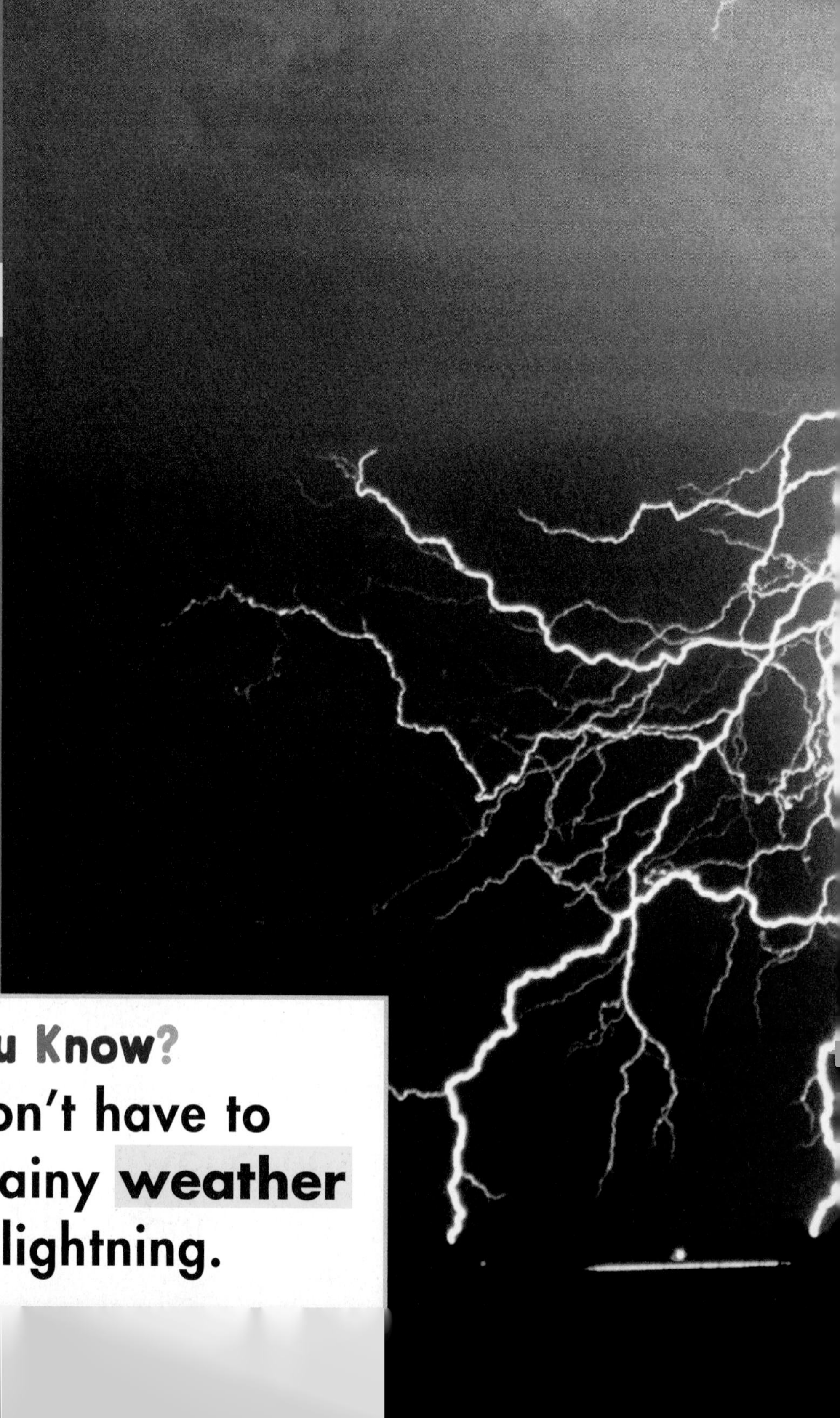

Vocabulary

weather
temperature
thermometer
wind
water vapor
evaporate
condense
water cycle

Did You Know?
You don't have to have rainy **weather** to get lightning.

Did You Know?
A landsailer can
go more than 100
miles an hour in
the wind.

What Is Weather?

Weather Conditions

You will need

paper

markers

1 Observe the changes in weather.

2 Draw or write what you observe.

3 Compare observations with a classmate. Add your page to a class book.

Science Skill

When you compare the things you observed, tell how they are the same and different.

Weather

It may be hot or cold outside. It may be sunny, cloudy, or rainy. All these words tell about weather. The **weather** is what the air outside is like.

rainy weather

Different Kinds of Weather

When the air outside changes, the weather changes. The weather may be hot one day and cool the next.

One day may be cloudy and rainy. The next day may be clear and sunny. One day may be very windy. Another day may be calm.

■ **How are these kinds of weather different?**

Meteorologist

People like to know what
the weather will be. They
check weather reports
made by a meteorologist. A meteorologist
is a scientist who studies weather.

Think About It

1. What is weather?
2. How can weather change
from day to day?

What Is Temperature?

Measuring Air Temperature

You will need

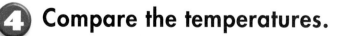

thermometer   paper and pencil   red crayon

1 Draw and label two thermometers.

2 Measure and record the air temperature in the classroom.

3 Put the thermometer outside for 5 minutes. Measure and record the air temperature.

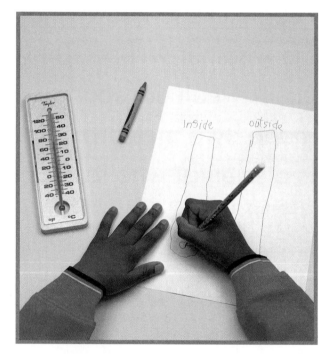

4 Compare the temperatures.

Science Skill

To measure temperature with a thermometer, read the number next to the top of the red line.

Temperature

The **temperature** is the measure of how hot or cold something is. Temperature is measured with a tool called a **thermometer**.

thermometer

■ **What is the temperature on the thermometer?**

Different Temperatures

The temperature of the air changes from day to day. It also changes as the seasons change. Sometimes it is so low that water freezes. Sometimes it is so high that an ice pop melts.

■ **How does the temperature change in these pictures?**

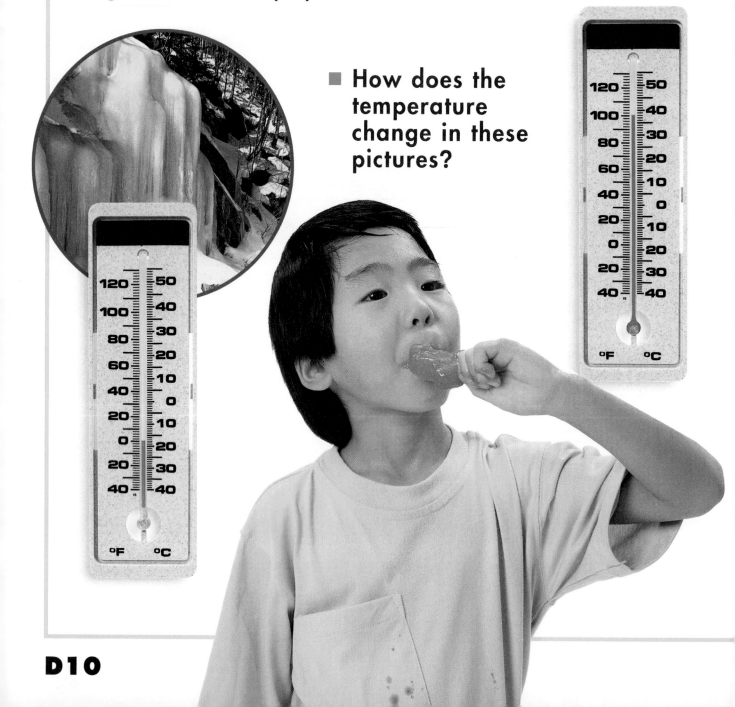

Air temperature may also change during the day. In the daytime the sun warms the air. The temperature goes up.

At night the sun does not warm the air. The temperature goes down, and the air feels cooler.

daytime

early evening

■ **How are the temperatures different here? Why?**

Think About It

1. What is a thermometer? How do you use it?

2. What is temperature? How does it change?

What Is Wind?

Wind Direction

You will need

drinking straw   round toothpick   paper triangle   tape

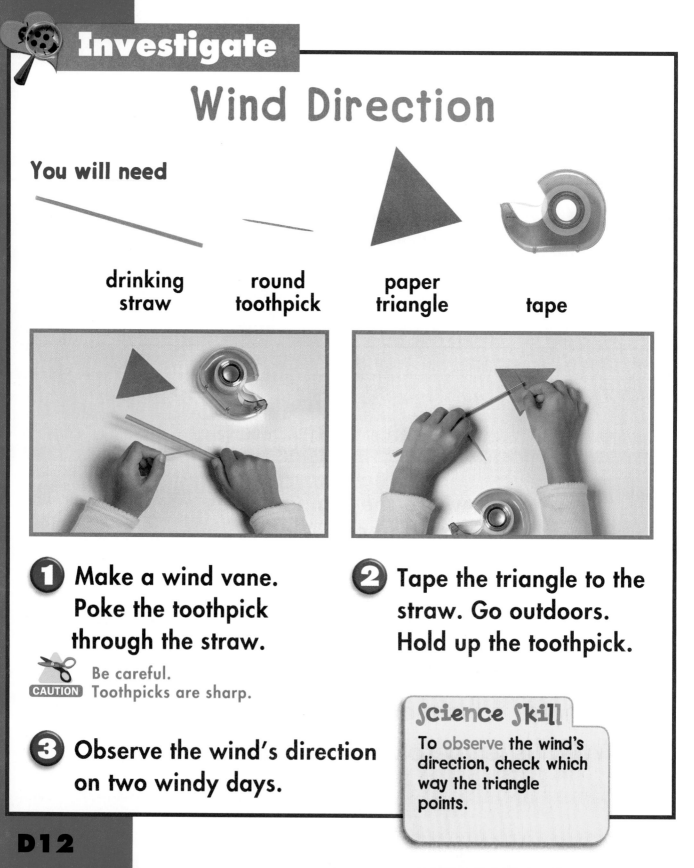

1 Make a wind vane. Poke the toothpick through the straw.

⚠ **CAUTION** Be careful. Toothpicks are sharp.

2 Tape the triangle to the straw. Go outdoors. Hold up the toothpick.

3 Observe the wind's direction on two windy days.

Science Skill

To observe the wind's direction, check which way the triangle points.

Wind

Moving air is called **wind**. Wind can push things. It can push a sailboat across a lake or blow a wind vane.

wind vane

N 2695

N-4139

Different Kinds of Wind

Sometimes the wind blows gently. Sometimes it blows hard.

A flag can show how hard the wind is blowing. When the wind blows gently, a flag ripples. When it blows hard, a flag flies straight out.

no wind	light wind	medium wind	strong wind

■ **How does a flag show how hard the wind is blowing?**

Strong wind turns windmills to make electricity. Sometimes wind can be too strong. The strong winds of a tornado can break up buildings.

Think About It

1. What is wind?
2. What are some different kinds of wind?

What Makes Clouds and Rain?

How Clouds Form

You will need

jar with lid

very warm water

ice cubes

1 Pour warm water into the jar. Wait. Pour out most of the water.

CAUTION Be careful. Water is hot!

2 Set the lid upside down on the jar. Observe the jar.

3 Put ice on the lid. Observe. Infer how clouds form.

Science Skill

To infer, first observe. Then think about what happened and draw a conclusion.

Clouds and Rain

Clouds are made up of many tiny drops of water. The drops may join and get heavier. When the drops get too heavy, they fall as rain.

The Water Cycle

Water moves from the Earth to the sky and back again in the **water cycle**.

2 Water vapor meets cooler air. It will then **condense**, or change into tiny drops of water. The drops form clouds.

1 The sun warms water and air. The water will **evaporate**, or change into water vapor.

Water vapor is water that you can not see in the air.

3 The water drops join and get heavier. They fall to Earth as rain, hail, sleet, or snow.

Think About It

1. How do clouds form?
2. How does rain form?

Measure Air Temperature

Monday

Tuesday

In some places the air temperature changes a lot from day to day. In other places it changes only a little.

Temperature Changes	
Day of Week	Degrees Fahrenheit
Monday	60
Tuesday	40
Wednesday	

Think and Do

Use a thermometer. Measure and record the temperature each day. Tell about the temperature changes.

Weather Sayings

Long ago, sailors looked for patterns to predict the weather. This is one of their sayings.

<u>Red sky</u> at night,
Sailors' delight.
<u>Red sky</u> at morning,
Sailors take warning.

Sailors observed that a red sunset often comes before a sunny day. A red sunrise often comes before a rainy day.

Think and Do

Observe the weather for a week. Look for patterns. Make up a weather saying about a pattern you observe.

Tell What You Know

1. Tell what you know about the diagram. Use the words *water cycle, water vapor, evaporate,* and *condense.*

Vocabulary

Use each word to tell about the picture.

2.

weather

3.

temperature

4.

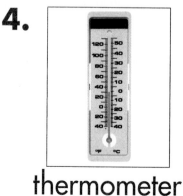

thermometer

5.

wind

Using Science Skills

6. **Compare** Make a chart about the weather. Observe and compare the weather in the morning and in the afternoon. Tell about the changes.

Today's Weather		
	Morning	Afternoon
How It Looks		
How It Sounds		
How It Feels		
How It Smells		

7. **Observe** Collect or draw pictures of clouds. Write a label for each picture.

Write a sentence that tells what each cloud looks like. Tell what weather you might have with that cloud.

2

The Seasons

Vocabulary

season

spring

summer

fall

winter

Did You Know?
Many parts of the world have four seasons, but the tropical rain forest only has one season.

Did You Know?

When it is **summer** in North America, it is **winter** in South America.

What Is Spring?

Investigate

What Helps Seeds Sprout

You will need

4 bean seeds

2 cups

mist bottle

paper towels

hand lens

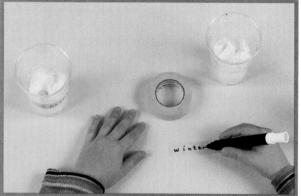

1 Put a damp paper towel in each cup. Add two seeds to each. Label the cups *winter* and *spring*.

2 Put the *winter* cup in a cold, dark place. Put the *spring* cup in a warm, dark place.

3 Observe the seeds with the hand lens three days later. What can you infer?

Science Skill
To infer, first observe, and then think about what you see.

Spring

A **season** is a time of year. **Spring** is the season that follows winter. In spring, there are more hours of daylight. The air gets warmer. Spring rains fall.

spring   summer   fall   winter

Plants and Animals in Spring

More daylight, warmer air, and spring rains help plants start growing. For farmers, spring is a good time to plant seeds.

■ **How does spring help these plants start growing?**

■ **Which are the young animals?**

Many animals give birth to their young in spring. Birds build nests and lay eggs. Lambs and other animals are born. The growing plants are food for many young animals.

Think About It

1. What is a season?
2. What is spring?

What Is Summer?

Investigate

Colors That Can Keep You Cool

You will need

4 thermometers

4 colors
of paper

stapler

clock

1 Fold and staple 4 color sheets of paper to make sleeves. Put a thermometer in each. Place in the sun.

2 Record the starting temperatures for each.

3 Wait 30 minutes. Record the temperatures again. Order from hottest to coolest.

Science Skill

To put the colors in order, start with the one with the hottest temperature. End with the coolest.

Summer

Summer is the season that follows spring. Summer has the most hours of daylight of any season. In many places the air gets hot.

spring summer fall winter

Plants and Animals in Summer

In summer, lots of sunlight helps plants grow leaves and flowers. Soon fruits begin to form and grow.

■ **What do these plants get in summer that helps them make fruit?**

In summer, young animals eat and grow. Young horses, called foals, become strong and fast.

Young birds lose their first feathers. They begin to look like adults.

Think About It

1. What is summer?
2. How is summer different from spring?

What Is Fall?

Storing Apples

You will need

apple rings

string

plastic bag

paper and pencil

1 Put some apple rings in the plastic bag. Store them on a shelf.

2 Hang the other apple rings on string. Don't let them touch.

3 Predict and record what will happen.

4 Wait one week. Record.

Science Skill

To predict which way to store apple rings is better, use what you know about food. Then decide.

Fall

The season that follows summer is **fall**. In fall, there are fewer hours of daylight. The air grows cool. In some places, leaves change colors and drop to the ground.

spring　　　summer　　　fall　　　winter

Plants and Animals in Fall

In fall, plants get less sunlight and stop growing bigger. They make seeds that will sprout next spring. Fruits and vegetables are ready to be picked.

■ **What made these plants stop growing bigger?**

When plants stop growing, animals have less food. Some animals move to places where there is more food. Others store food so they have something to eat in winter.

Think About It

1. What is fall?
2. How is fall different from summer?

What Is Winter?

Investigate

Keeping Warm in Cold Weather

You will need

plastic bag

container of ice water

things to keep your hand warm

1 Put your hand in the bag. Then put your hand in the ice water. Does the bag keep your hand warm?

2 What could you put in the bag to keep your hand warm? Choose some things to try.

3 Investigate your ideas by trying them. Which one works best?

Science Skill

To investigate how to keep your hand warm, try out each of your ideas.

Winter

Winter is the season that follows fall. There are fewer hours of daylight than in fall. In many places the air gets cold and snow falls.

spring • summer • fall • winter

Plants and Animals in Winter

In winter, days do not have many hours of sunlight. The branches of many trees and bushes are bare.

Some plants are resting. Some plants that made seeds are now dead.

Where winters are cold, animals can not find much food. Some eat food they stored in fall.

■ How do these animals meet their needs for food in winter?

Think About It

1. What is winter?
2. What are some ways animals live in winter?

Art Link

A Photographer Observes the Seasons

Ansel Adams was a photographer. Each season, he took pictures of his favorite places. His photographs help us see the beauty of the seasons.

fall

winter

Think and Do

Think of your favorite place. Draw pictures to show it in different seasons. Label each picture with the season it shows.

Read a Graph

In a part of northern California, some seasons are wet and some are dry. This graph shows about how many inches of rain fall in each season.

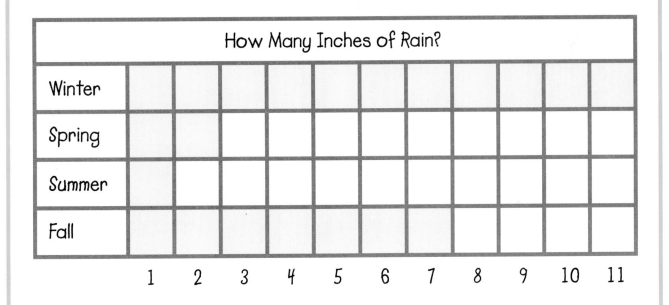

How Many Inches of Rain?

	1	2	3	4	5	6	7	8	9	10	11
Winter											
Spring											
Summer											
Fall											

Think and Do

Look at the bar graph. Which season is the wettest in northern California? Which is the driest?

Tell What You Know

1. Tell what you know about the pictures. Use the word *spring*, *summer*, *fall*, or *winter* to tell about each one.

Vocabulary

Use each word to tell about the picture.

2.

season

3.

spring

4.

summer

5.

fall

6.

winter

Using Science Skills

7. **Order** Use four sheets of paper. On each, write the name of one of the seasons. Then draw the clothes you would wear. Put your sheets in order, beginning with summer.

8. **Predict and Investigate** Look at the colors of these shirts. Predict which color will stay the coolest in hot sun. Write your prediction. Use any color paper to investigate your idea.

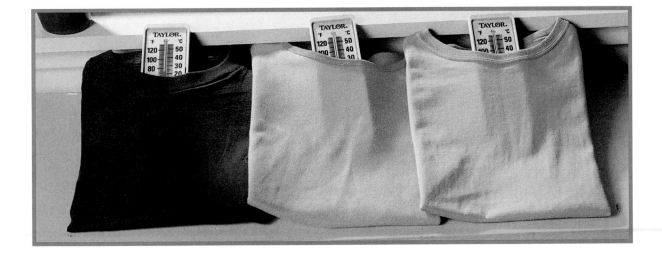

Make a Sail for a Car

Put a paper sail on a toy car. Blow on the sail to make the car move. What could you do to make a better sail? Try your ideas.

Investigate Water Vapor

1. With an adult present, blow into a small plastic bag.

2. Observe the water drops inside. They come from the water vapor in your breath.

3. Put the bag in a freezer for five minutes. Tell what happens.

4. Put the bag in the sun for five minutes. Tell what happens.

Make a Four Seasons Poster

Fold a big sheet of paper into four parts. Label each part for a different season. Add pictures of things you like to do in each season. Talk about your poster.

Find Seasons in a Closet

What clothes do people wear at different times of the year where you live? Brainstorm ideas. Write a list that shows at least two things for each season.

WRITING

Flap Facts Make a flap book about the seasons. Under each flap, tell one thing about that season.

READING

Animal Seasons
by Brian Wildsmith
Read about ways plants and animals change with the seasons. Talk about how the weather changes.

 COMPUTER CENTER
Visit *The Learning Site* at
www.harcourtschool.com

Matter and Energy

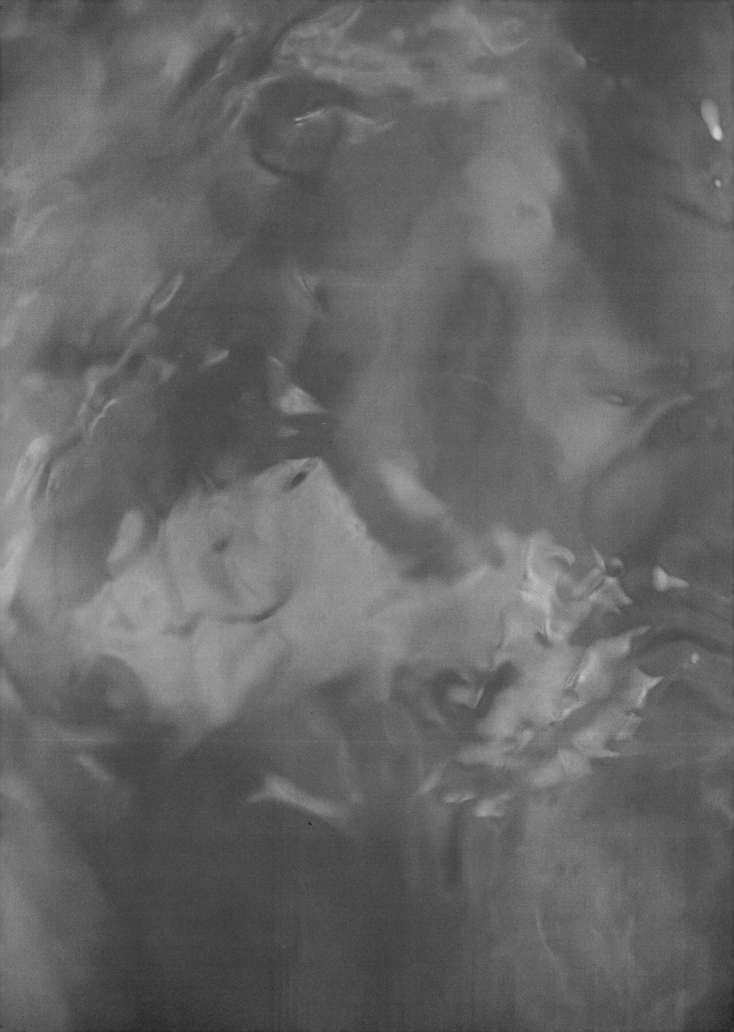

Physical Science

Matter and Energy

UNIT PROJECT

Show Time!

Practice making shadow puppets. Give a puppet show about heat and light.

CHAPTER 1

Investigate Matter

Vocabulary

solid
matter
liquid
float
sink
gas
change
mechanic

Did You Know?
Boats **float** higher in salt water than they do in fresh water.

Did You Know?

Some liquids **sink** in other liquids.

What Can We Observe About Solids?

Solid Objects

You will need

objects   paper and pencil

1 Observe each object.

2 Compare the sizes, shapes, and colors of the objects.

3 Think of three ways to classify the objects. Draw or write them on your paper.

Science Skill

To classify the objects, find ways they are the same and group them.

Matter and Solids

Everything around you is **matter**.
Toys and blocks are matter. You are, too!

- **What matter do you see?**

Observing Solids

Some matter is solid. A **solid** is matter that keeps its shape. It keeps its shape even when you move it.

■ **How do you know these toys are solids?**

Sorting Solids

You can sort solids in many ways. You can sort toys by color. This graph shows how many toys of each color there are.

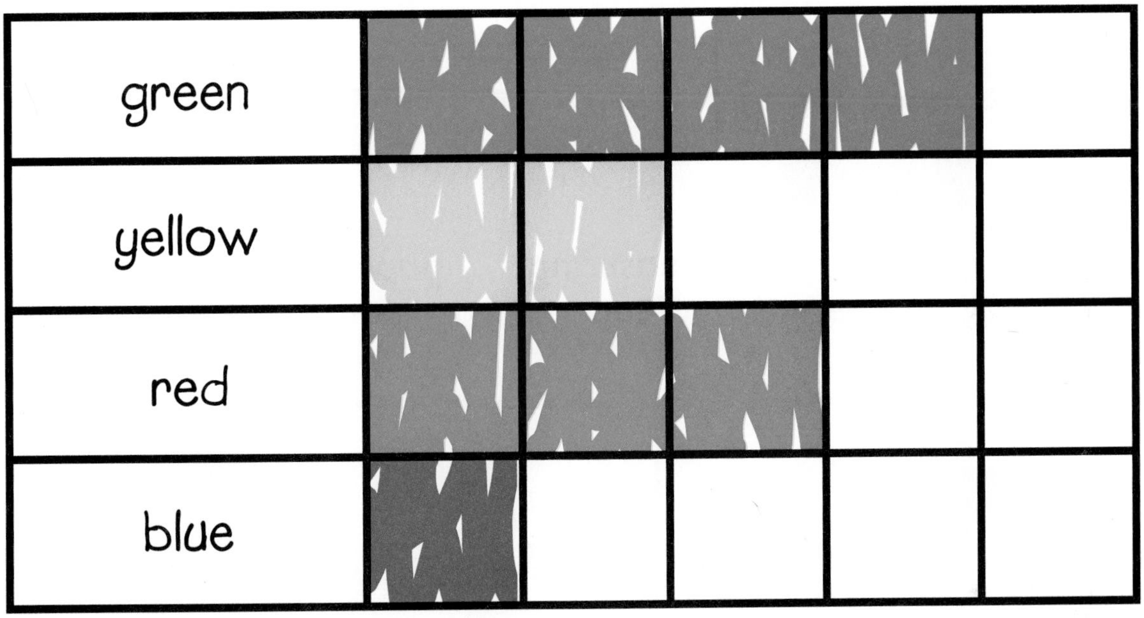

green					
yellow					
red					
blue					

■ **What other ways could you sort the toys in the toy box?**

Think About It

1. What is matter?

2. What is a solid?

What Can We Observe About Liquids?

Liquids in Bottles

You will need

3 containers

measuring cup

paper and pencil

1 Draw the shape of the water in each container.

2 Which container do you think has the most water?

3 Measure the water. Write a number for each container. Use the numbers to tell what you found out.

Science Skill

You can write numbers when you measure. Use the numbers to compare the things you measured.

Liquids

Matter that flows is called a **liquid**. A liquid does not have a shape of its own. It takes the shape of the container you pour it into.

Observing Liquids

Some liquids, like water, are thin. Others are thick. Some liquids mix with water. Some, such as oil, do not mix with water.

Thin liquids flow quickly. Thick liquids flow slowly. This pan has dish soap, honey, and juice running down it.

Which Liquid Flows Fastest?	
Liquid	Time
dish soap	9 seconds
honey	47 seconds
juice	1 second

■ **Read the chart. Which liquid flows fastest?**

Think About It

1. What is a liquid?

2. What can we observe about liquids?

What Objects Sink or Float?

 Investigate

Shapes That Sink or Float

You will need

ball of clay   aquarium with water   paper and pencil

1 Gather data about shapes that sink or float. Put the clay ball in the water.

2 Record data about what happens.

3 Make the clay into different shapes. Do they sink or float? Record.

Science Skill

When you gather data, you observe things. When you record data, you write and draw what you observe.

Objects That Sink or Float

Some objects **float**, or stay on top of a liquid. Others **sink**, or drop to the bottom of a liquid. You can change the shape of some objects to make them float or sink.

Floaters and Sinkers

Some objects have shapes that help them float. Others have shapes that make them sink.

You can not always guess which objects will float. You must test them to find out.

You can group objects as floaters or sinkers. What objects here would you put into these two groups? Why?

Think About It

1. What do *float* and *sink* mean?
2. What helps an object sink or float?

What Can We Observe About Gases?

Air in a Bottle

You will need

balloon

plastic soft drink bottle

1 Squeeze the bottle to observe the air in it. Blow up the balloon. Feel the air come out.

2 Put the balloon in the bottle. Pull the end over the top.

3 Try to blow up the balloon. What else is in the bottle? Draw a conclusion.

Science Skill

To draw a conclusion about what happened, think about what you observed.

Gases

Gases are matter. A **gas** does not have a shape of its own. It spreads out to fill its container and take its shape.

How Can We Change Objects?

Changing Paper

You will need

4 cards with slits   paints and brushes   glitter   glue   paper and pencil

1 Observe the cards. Record how they look and feel.

2 How could you change the way the cards look and feel? Investigate your ideas.

3 Record how you change the cards.

Science Skill

To investigate, think of changes you could make, and then try them out.

Changing Objects

You can **change** objects, or make them different. You can change their shape, size, color, or texture.

Observing Changes

You can change objects in different ways. You can roll or bend some objects to change their shape.

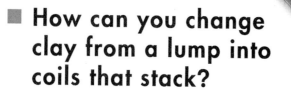

■ **How can you change clay from a lump into coils that stack?**

You can change some liquids by freezing them. Freezing changes fruit juice into a frozen ice pop.

You can change an object by mixing it with other things. You might make a rock animal for fun. It might be a mix of the rock, paint, and other things.

■ How did someone change this rock to look like a spider?

Think About It

1. What are some things you can change about objects?

2. What are three things you can do to objects to change them?

What Happens When Objects Are Taken Apart?

Wheels and an Axle

You will need

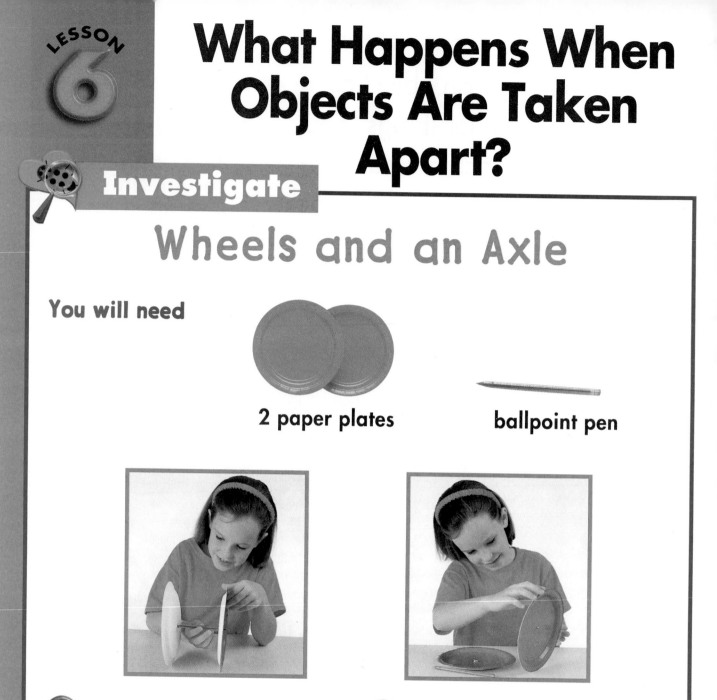

2 paper plates

ballpoint pen

1 Make a model of two wheels and an axle. Poke the pen through the plates. Do the plate wheels roll?

Be careful. The pen point is sharp!

2 Take apart the wheels and axle. Do the wheels roll? Draw a conclusion.

Science Skill

When you make a model of something, you can use it to find out how the real thing works.

Objects and Their Parts

Many objects are made of parts.
The parts work together to make the
objects work. Without all their parts,
many objects will not work.

How Parts Work Together

A camera must have film to work. Without film, you can not take photographs. A plane must have fuel to fly. Without fuel, the plane's engine will not run.

Sometimes a car does not work the way it should. A **mechanic** can fix a broken part or put in a new one. Then the car will work the way it should again.

Think About It

1. What happens when objects do not have all their parts?
2. What does a mechanic do if a car part is broken?

Art Link

Mixing Objects to Make Art

A Spanish artist named Pablo Picasso made this sculpture. He used two everyday objects to show something new. Look at the bicycle seat and handlebars.

- **How does this art look like a bull's head?**

Bull's Head by Pablo Picasso

 **Think** and **Do**

Choose two or three objects in your classroom. Plan a way to put them together to show something new. Then follow your plan.

 **Math Link**

How Much Can Ships Carry?

Big ships can carry heavy cargo. On the left you see a ship with no cargo. The red line shows that it is floating high in the water. On the right you see a ship loaded with cargo. You can not see the red line. The ship is floating lower in the water.

Think and Do

Make a foil boat. Put it in the water. Slowly put pennies in your boat. How many pennies can it carry without sinking?

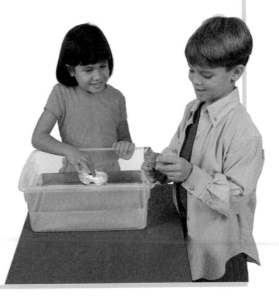

Tell What You Know

1. Use the word *solid*, *liquid*, or *gas* to tell about each picture.

Vocabulary

Use each word to tell about the picture.

2.

matter

3.

float

4.

sink

5.

change

6.

mechanic

Using Science Skills

7. Gather and Record Data
Make a chart to gather and record data about liquids. Put one drop of water and one drop of oil on wax paper.

Liquids				
	Makes a Round Drop	Makes a Flat Drop	Can Be Dragged	Can Not Be Dragged
Water				
Oil				

Observe each drop. Use a toothpick to drag each one. Try other liquids and add them to the chart.

8. Draw a Conclusion Think about what makes these cars roll. Draw a conclusion about why one car rolled farther.

CHAPTER 2

Heat and Light

Nothing

Vocabulary

heat
melt
prism
refract
reflect

Did You Know?
The blue part of
a flame gives off
the most **heat**.

Did You Know?
Your hand gives off enough heat to <mark>melt</mark> some solids.

What Is Heat?

Investigate

What Heat Does to Water

You will need

2 cups with water

2 thermometers

paper and pencil

clock

1 Measure the temperature of the water in each cup.

2 Make a chart. Write a number to show each temperature.

3 Wait 10 minutes. Read and record each temperature.

4 Draw a conclusion.

Science Skill

Use numbers to tell what you found out. Compare the numbers. Draw a conclusion.

Heat

Heat can make things warmer. The sun gives off heat. The sun's heat warms the Earth's land, air, and water.

Other Things That Give Off Heat

Fire also gives off heat. Heat from a fire warms the people sitting around it.

■ **How is the fire being used in this picture?**

Rubbing Makes Heat

Almost anything gives off heat if you rub it. Try rubbing your hands together. Can you feel the heat they give off?

■ **What is this boy doing to make heat?**

Think About It

1. What does heat do?
2. What are some things that give off heat?

How Does Heat Change Matter?

How Heat Changes Water

You will need

| food coloring | hot water in a bowl | cold water in a bowl | paper and pencil |

1 Gather data about how heat changes water. Put a drop of food coloring in cold water. Record.

2 Put a drop of food coloring in hot water. Record.

 Be careful. Hot!
CAUTION

3 How did heat change the water? Tell what you found out.

Science Skill

To gather data about something, observe it. Then draw or write to record your observations.

Learn About

How Heat Changes Matter

Heat changes matter. It makes a solid melt and a liquid evaporate. It makes a gas spread out.

■ How is the sun's heat changing this snowperson?

What Heat Does to Matter

You can observe what heat does to matter. You can heat solids such as ice or sugar to melt them. When solids **melt**, they turn into liquids.

You can heat a liquid, such as soup. Some of it will evaporate, or change to a gas.

■ **What does heat do to these solids and liquids?**

You can heat a gas, such as air.
Hot air spreads out to fill this balloon.

Think About It

1. How does heat change a solid like ice?
2. How does heat change liquids and gases?

What Is Light?

Light and Color

You will need

prism

objects

paper and pencil

crayons or markers

flashlight

1 Shine a light. Look at objects through the prism.

2 Draw a picture of what you observe. Label it with the colors you observe.

3 Use your picture to communicate what you observed.

Science Skill

To communicate, use the labeled picture to talk about what you observed.

Light

Light lets us see. The sun gives off
light as well as heat. The sun's light
helps us see what is around us.

Other Things That Give Off Light

Many things besides the sun give off both light and heat. We can use their light to see when there is no sunlight.

■ What are some things that give off both light and heat?

Light and Color

Light is made of colors. You can see the colors when light passes through a prism. A **prism** is any clear object that breaks light into colors.

prism

Think About It

1. What does light do?
2. When can you see the colors light is made of?

What Can Light Do?

Investigate

Making Light Bounce

You will need

flashlight with battery

index card in clay

mirror

1 Turn the flashlight on. Observe the light.

2 Put the mirror in front of the light. Move the mirror. Observe.

3 Investigate this problem. How can you make light shine on the card without moving the card?

Science Skill

To investigate a problem, you plan and try different ideas.

How Light Moves

Light moves in a straight line until it hits a solid or a liquid. Dust in the air helps us see light's straight lines.

What Light Can Do

When light hits something solid, it **reflects**, or bounces off in a new direction.

Light reflecting off a cat lets us see the cat. The cat's shadow shows where the cat blocks the light.

■ **What makes the cat's shadow?**

Light passes through water as well as air. Light may bend, or **refract**, where water and air meet. An object that is partly in water may look bent.

■ What happens to light when it hits a mirror?

Think About It

1. In what way does light move?
2. What can light do?

Social Studies/Career Link

A Hot Air Balloonist Explores

Jetta Schantz flies hot air balloons. To go up, she heats the air in her balloon. The hot air in it spreads out and gets lighter. The cool air pushes it up and lifts the balloon.

Think and Do

Observe how hot air spreads out. Blow up a balloon about halfway, and tie it. Use a string to measure around it. Hold the balloon in hot water for a few minutes. Measure again.

Math Link

Measure Shadows

Children in many places have fun with shadows. Children in Indonesia make deer shadow puppets. They sing songs about what their puppets do.

 **Think and Do**

With a partner, make shadow puppets on paper. How can you make them smaller or larger? Trace two shadows. Measure them with paper clips. Find the difference between the two.

Tell What You Know

1. Use the word *light* or *heat* to tell about each picture.

Vocabulary

Tell which picture goes with each word.

a.   **b.**

2. prism

3. refract

4. melt

5. reflect

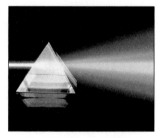

c.   **d.**

Using Science Skills

6. Gather Data Does a foam cup or a metal cup keep cocoa hotter over time? Gather your own data, or read the data in the chart. Use the data to decide which cup to use.

Which Cup Keeps Cocoa Hotter?			
Kind of Cup	Temperature at Start	After 5 Minutes	After 10 Minutes
Foam Cup	55 degrees Celsius	49 degrees Celsius	47 degrees Celsius
Metal Cup	55 degrees Celsius	47 degrees Celsius	43 degrees Celsius

7. Use Numbers Tape two mirrors together. Put a small object between them. Count how many times you see the object. Then move the mirrors. Make them show the object only once.

Make Juice Bars

Change liquid juice into a solid by making juice pops.

1. Have a family member help you pour fruit juice into an ice cube tray.

2. Put a toothpick into each part of the tray. *Be careful. Toothpicks are sharp.*

3. Freeze and eat!

Floating Drops

1. Fill jar with salad oil.

2. Put two or three drops of food coloring into the oil. Put the lid on the jar.

3. Tip the jar. What happens to the colored drops? Talk about what floats and why.

Be a Shadow Tracker

1. In the morning, put a sheet of paper by a sunny window.

2. Put a stick in a ball of clay on the paper. Trace the stick's shadow. Write the time.

3. Trace the shadow and write the time again two more times that day.

4. Tell what happens to the shadow.

What Keeps Cold In?

1. Put one ice cube in a foam cup. Put another foam cup on top of that cup.

2. Do the same thing using two clear plastic cups.

3. Put both sets of cups in a warm place.

4. Observe the ice cubes in one hour. Which cups would you use to keep a drink cold?

Water is a liquid.

WRITING

Tab Book On separate sheets of paper, write about solids, liquids, and gases. Add a label to each page. Put your pages together to make a book.

READING

Day Light, Night Light
by Franklyn M. Branley
Read about different places light comes from. Find the page that shows heat about to change a solid.

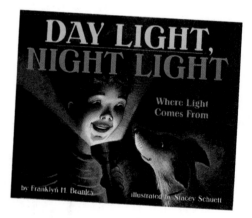

COMPUTER CENTER
Visit *The Learning Site* at
www.harcourtschool.com

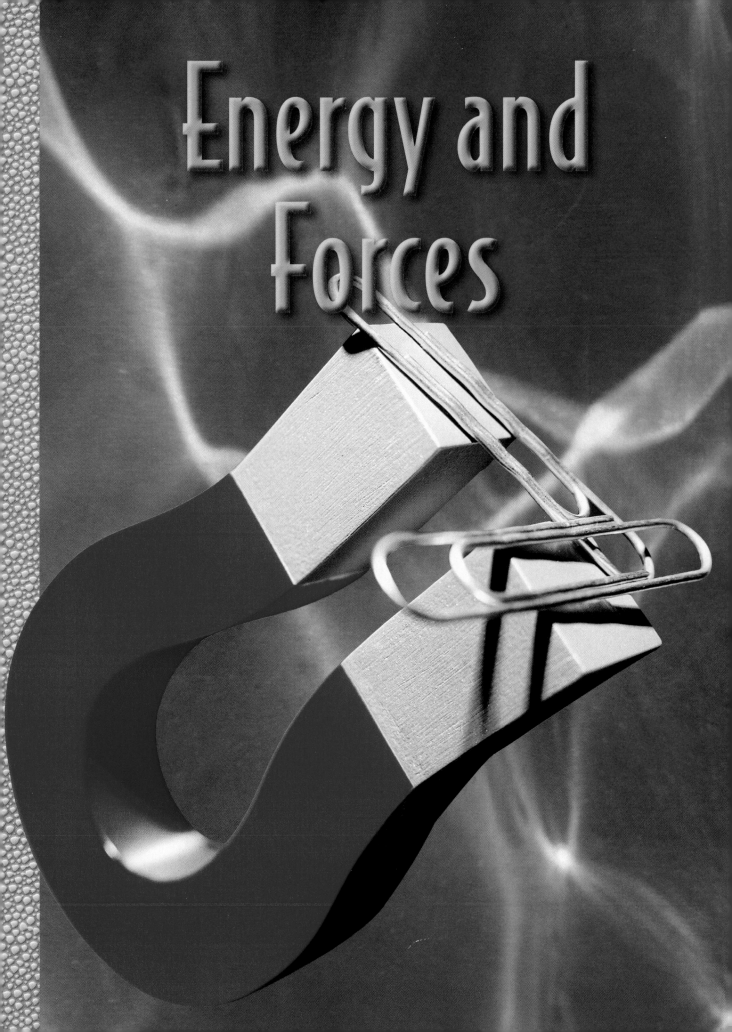

Energy and Forces

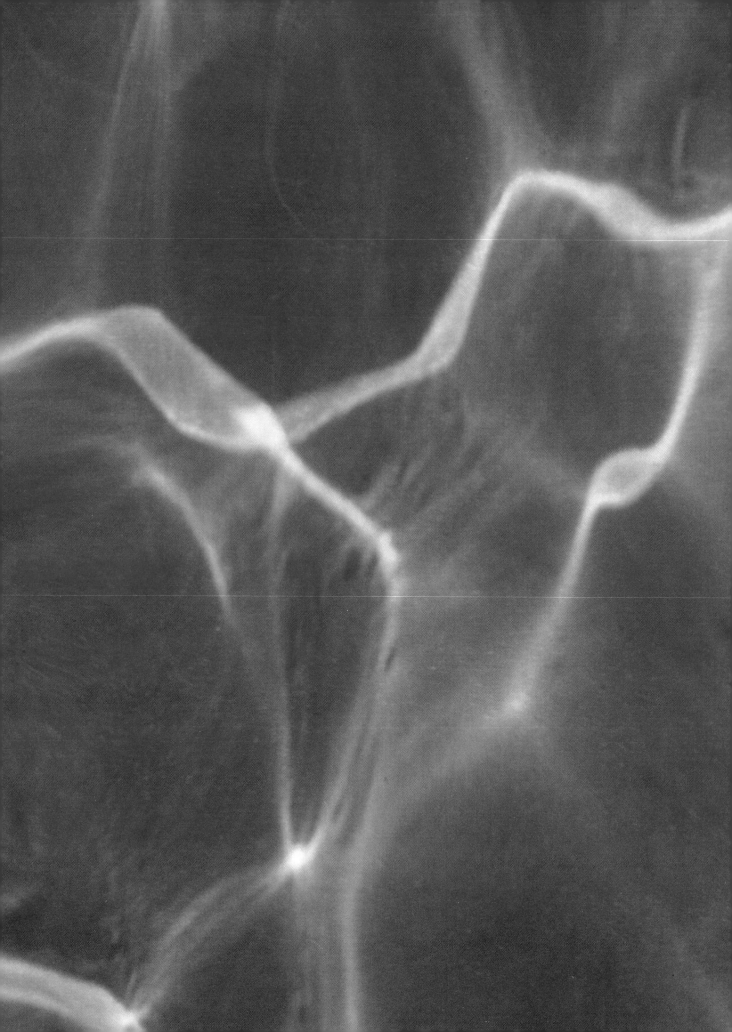

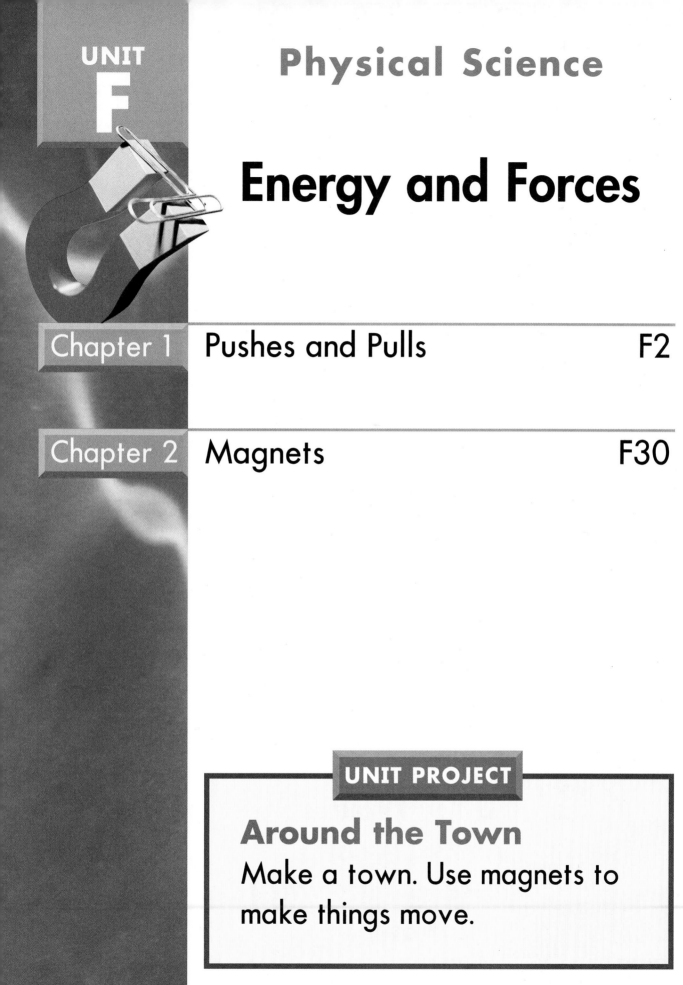

UNIT F

Physical Science

Energy and Forces

UNIT PROJECT

Around the Town

Make a town. Use magnets to make things move.

Pushes and Pulls

Vocabulary

force
push
pull
zigzag
motion
surface
friction
wheel

Did You Know?
Tree roots can **push** a rock when they grow.

Did You Know?

The golden wheel spider can roll like a **wheel**.

What Makes Things Move?

Pushes and Pulls

You will need

small block

things to make
the block move

paper
and pencil

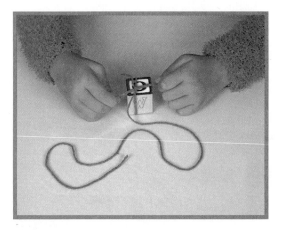

1 What could you do to push or pull the block?

2 Write a plan to investigate your ideas. Then follow your plan.

3 Tell what you used to move the block. Use the word *push* or *pull*.

Science Skill

You investigate by thinking of ideas and trying them out.

Making Things Move

A **force** is a push or a pull. When you **push** something, you press it away. When you **pull** something, you tug it closer.

push

pull

Pushes and Pulls

Pushes and pulls make things move or stop moving. A tow truck pulls a car to the repair shop. A player pushes with a glove to stop a moving ball.

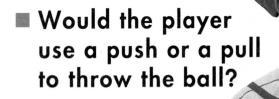

■ **Would the player use a push or a pull to throw the ball?**

A push or a pull can make something change direction. When you kick a ball, you are using a push. First the ball rolls to you. Your push makes it change direction. Then it moves away from you.

■ **What will the ball do when the player kicks it?**

Think About It

1. What is a force?

2. What can pushes and pulls do?

What Are Some Ways Things Move?

Investigate

Moving Objects

You will need

objects

paper and pencil

1 Observe and record how each object moves when you push or pull it.

2 Group objects that move the same way. Write how you grouped them.

Science Skill

To group the objects, put those that move in the same way together.

Ways Things Move

Pushes and pulls make things move in different ways. Tell what you know about how these rides move.

Telling How Things Move

There are different ways to tell how things move. One way is by the path they make. A car moves in a straight path. A skier may **zigzag**, or make sharp turns back and forth.

Another way to tell how things move is by their speed. Two bikers may start at the same time. If one moves ahead, he or she is moving faster.

Some things move the same way over and over. A top spins round and round. A swing moves back and forth.

■ **What kind of force keeps a swing moving?**

Think About It

1. What are some ways things move?
2. How can you tell if one thing is moving faster than another?

Why Do Things Move the Way They Do?

 Investigate

Predicting Motion

You will need

ramp   plastic ball   tape   block

1 Set up the ramp. Predict where the ball will stop. Mark that place with tape.

2 Let the ball roll down the ramp. Was your prediction right?

3 Now put the block where the ball will hit it. Do Step 2 again.

Science Skill

To predict where the ball will stop, think about how a ball rolls and bounces.

Why Things Move the Way They Do

Moving from one place to another is **motion**. You can observe the motion of an object. This will help you predict where it will move next.

Changing Motion

A push or pull can change the motion of something. A hockey puck moves straight ahead unless something changes its motion.

Different kinds of pushes change how far the puck moves. A hard push moves the puck far. A gentle push moves it only a short way.

■ **What kind of push should the player use to move the puck a short way?**

Changing Direction

A force can change the direction in which an object moves. A ball will roll in one direction until something pushes it and makes it change.

■ What does the paddle do to the ball in table tennis?

Bumps are the pushes that change the direction of bumper boats. When you bump your boat against another boat, your boat bounces back.

Think About It

1. What is motion?
2. What can change the motion of something?

How Do Objects Move on Surfaces?

Investigate

Smooth and Rough Surfaces

You will need

ramp

toy truck

meterstick

paper and pencil

1 Set up a ramp on a smooth surface. Let the truck roll down.

2 Measure how far it rolls. Record the number. Do the same on a rough surface.

3 On which surface does the truck roll farther? Use your numbers to tell.

Science Skill

Measure how far the truck rolls from the end of the ramp to where the truck stops.

Different Surfaces

A **surface** is the top or outside of something. This floor has both a smooth surface and a rough surface. The truck moves in a different way on each surface.

More Friction, Less Friction

When two surfaces rub together, they make friction. **Friction** is a force that makes it harder to move things.

A rough surface makes more friction than a smooth one. On a rough road, a bike is harder to move. You have to push harder on the pedals.

■ **What surfaces rub together when you ride a bike over a road?**

You can change how much friction a surface makes. If you cover a surface with something wet, it makes less friction. If you cover a surface with something rough, it makes more friction.

Think About It

1. What is friction?
2. What kind of surface makes more friction? What kind makes less friction?

How Do Wheels Help Objects Move?

Investigate

Rollers

You will need

rollers

heavy book

toy truck

tape

1 Push the book. Then put rollers under it. Push again. Which is easier?

2 Push the truck. Tape the wheels, and push it again. Which is easier?

3 Draw a conclusion about wheels and rollers.

Science Skill

To draw a conclusion about something, use what you have observed to explain what happens.

What Wheels Can Do

A roller is any object that rolls. A **wheel** is a roller that turns on an axle. Rollers and wheels make things easier to push or pull.

Many Ways to Use Wheels

People use wheels in many ways. They use baskets on wheels to carry things when they shop. They use chairs on wheels to help them move around. Some children put wheels on boxes to make play cars.

People use wheels to help them push or pull loads. A dolly's wheels make it easy to push heavy boxes. Many suitcases have wheels so that people can pull them along.

■ **Why do people use things that have wheels?**

Think About It

1. What is a wheel?

2. What can wheels do?

An Architect Plans Buildings

I. M. Pei designs buildings. He knows about forces that push and pull. He designs buildings that won't fall down.

Think and Do

Use index cards to build a house. Then blow on your house of cards. Find different ways to make a house you can not blow down.

Push for Points

In some games, players use pushes to score points. Air hockey and bowling are two games like this.

Think and Do

Make a game that uses pushes to score points. Use a box lid. Then use a pencil to flip a bottle cap ten times into the lid.

Add the number it lands on to your score each time.

Tell What You Know

1. Tell what you know about the picture. Use the words *force*, *motion*, *surface*, and *friction*.

Vocabulary

Tell which picture goes with each word.

2. push
3. pull
4. zigzag
5. wheel

a.

b.

c.

d.

Using Science Skills

6. Measure Pull a rock across rough and smooth surfaces with a rubber band. Measure how long the rubber band stretches each time. Make a chart. Record the numbers. Which makes more friction?

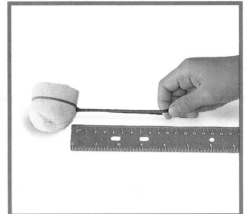

Friction on Surfaces	
Surface	How Long the Rubber Band Stretches
rough	
smooth	

7. Draw a Conclusion Rub your hands together. Feel the friction. Then put a few drops of oil on your hands. Rub again. Draw a conclusion.

CHAPTER 2

Magnets

Vocabulary

magnet

attract

strength

repel

poles

magnetic force

magnetize

Did You Know?
The Maglev train is run by **magnets**.

Did You Know?
These magnets can **repel** each other.

F31

What Are Magnets?

What a Magnet Can Do

You will need

bar magnet

objects

paper and pencil

What a Magnet Can Do		
Object	Pulls	Does Not Pull

1 Gather data about the magnet. Hold it near each object.

2 Make a chart like this one. Record what you observe.

3 Group the objects the magnet pulls and those it does not pull.

Science Skill

To gather data about what a magnet can do, observe and record what it does.

Magnets

A **magnet** is a piece of iron that can **attract**, or pull, things. The things it pulls must also be made of iron. Iron is a kind of metal.

■ **How are magnets used here?**

How People Use Magnets

People use magnets to hold things closed and to lift things. They also use them in televisions and electric motors.

A farmer may put a magnet in a cow's stomach. The magnet attracts bits of metal that the cow may eat. This keeps the metal from hurting the cow.

cow
magnet

Where Magnets Can Be Found

Some magnets are found in nature. Lodestone is a kind of magnet found in the ground.

lodestone

■ How are the children using magnets in this fishing game?

How Magnets Are the Same and Different

Magnets are the same in one way. They attract objects made of iron. They do not attract objects made of other materials.

Magnets may be different in other ways. They may be round or square, big or small, straight or curved. They may be different colors.

Magnets may be different in **strength**, or how strongly they pull. One magnet may attract more paper clips than another.

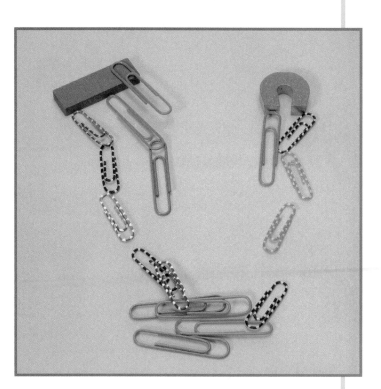

■ **Look at the chart. Which magnet has the greater strength?**

Magnet Strength	
Magnet	Number of Clips
bar magnet	6
horseshoe magnet	3

Think About It

1. What is a magnet?
2. What are some ways people use magnets?

What Are the Poles of a Magnet?

A Magnet's Ends

You will need

bar magnet   paper clips   paper and pencil

1 Pick up paper clips with one end of the magnet. Record the number. Then do the other end.

2 Pick up paper clips with the middle of the magnet. Record the number.

3 Make a bar graph. Infer which parts of the magnet are strongest.

Science Skill

To infer which parts of the magnet are the strongest, compare the numbers in your bar graph.

The Poles of a Magnet

A magnet has two **poles**. These are the places where its pulling force is strongest. Where are the poles of this bar magnet? How can you tell?

What Poles Can Do

Every magnet has a north pole and a south pole. They are often called the *N* pole and the *S* pole.

Two poles that are different attract each other. An *N* pole and an *S* pole attract each other.

Two poles that are the same **repel**, or push away, each other. Two *N* poles repel each other.

■ **What do you think two *S* poles would do?**

Bits of iron can show where a magnet's pull is strongest. The iron bits make a pattern around the magnet. More bits go to the poles, where the pull is strongest.

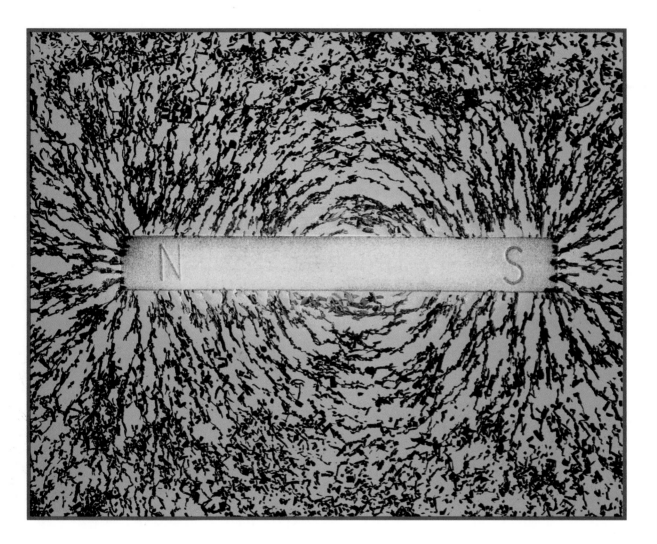

Think About It

1. What are poles?
2. What do poles do?

What Can a Magnet Pull Through?

Things Magnets Pull Through

You will need

bar magnet

paper clips

different materials

1 Can a magnet attract paper clips through things? Plan an investigation to find out. Write your plan.

2 Follow your plan to investigate your ideas. Record what you observe.

3 Use your data to communicate what you find out.

Science Skill

To investigate what things a magnet can pull through, first make a plan and then try your ideas.

The Force of a Magnet

A magnet's pull is called **magnetic force**. This force can pass through some things to attract iron objects.

■ **What material is magnetic force passing through to attract these puppets?**

Observing Magnetic Force

The magnetic force of a magnet can pass through paper. It can also pass through water and glass.

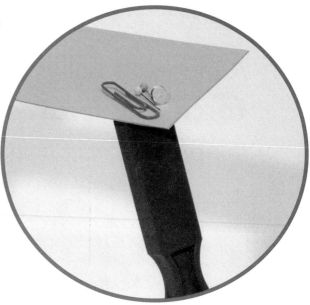

■ **What do you think might happen if the glass were thicker?**

Magnetic force is strong close to a magnet. It can pull a paper clip through the air. Farther away, it may not be strong enough to do this.

Think About It

1. What is magnetic force?
2. What are some materials magnetic force can pass through?

How Can You Make a Magnet?

Making a Magnet

You will need

magnet

2 paper clips

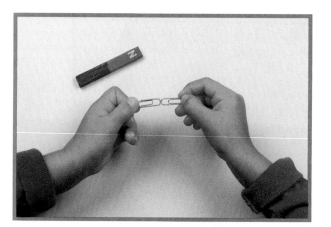

1 Touch one clip to the other. Observe.

2 Use the magnet to pick up one clip. Touch that clip to the other one. Observe.

3 Take away the magnet. Draw a conclusion. How can you make a magnet?

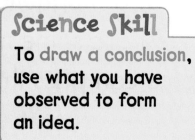

Science Skill

To draw a conclusion, use what you have observed to form an idea.

Making a Magnet

A magnet can **magnetize**, or give magnetic force to, things it attracts. The magnet on this crane has magnetized some pieces of metal. Their new magnetic force attracts more pieces.

Ways to Make a Magnet

You can magnetize an iron nail. Stroke the nail on the magnet ten times the same way. Then the nail will be magnetized for a short time.

■ **How can you tell that this nail is now a magnet?**

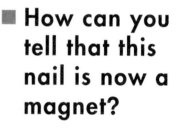

Some magnets are made from iron heated with other materials. These magnets are made in a factory.

Magnet Engineer

A magnet engineer finds new ways to make magnets. These magnets may be stronger or last longer than iron ones.

Think About It

1. What can you use to magnetize an object made of iron?
2. How can you make a magnet?

Math Link

Measure Magnetic Force

You can compare the strengths of different magnets. To do this, you will need to record how far their magnetic forces reach.

Think and Do

Lay a paper clip at one end of a paper strip. Hold one magnet at the other end. Slide the magnet slowly toward the clip. Make a mark to show where the magnet is when the clip moves.

Do the same thing with each magnet. Which magnet is the strongest?

Compass Readings

Long ago, travelers used compasses to find their way. Travelers still use them today. A compass has a magnetized needle that always points north.

Think and Do

Make your own compass. Float a plastic plate in water. Place a bar magnet in the center of the plate. Turn the plate. Which way is north?

Tell What You Know

1. Use the words *strength*, *poles*, and *magnetic force* to tell about each picture.

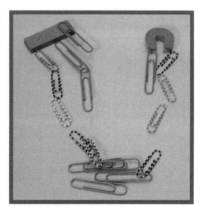

Vocabulary

Tell which picture goes with each word.

2. magnet

3. attract

4. repel

5. magnetize

a.

b.

c.

d.

Using Science Skills

6. Infer Look at the two patterns made by the bits of iron. Which magnet made each pattern? How do you know?

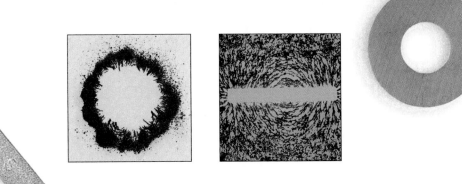

7. Investigate Some people use a metal detector to help them find things made of metal.

Play a metal detector game. Ask a partner to put three metal objects in a group of objects.

Predict which objects your magnet will attract. Investigate to find out.

Magnetic Kite

1. Cut out a tissue paper kite.

2. Attach thread and a paper clip.

3. Tape the thread's tail to a table.

4. Use the magnet to pick up your kite without touching it.

Magnetic Race-Car Game

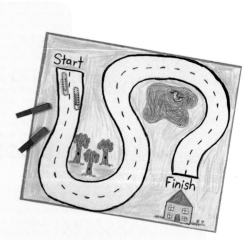

1. Draw a road on cardboard.

2. Put two paper clips on the road.

3. Put two magnets under the cardboard. Move the magnets to race your clips.

Make a Water Wheel

1. Push toothpicks into the ends of a piece of clay. *Be careful. Toothpicks are sharp.*

2. Push strips cut from a carton into the clay to make a water wheel.

3. Hold the wheel by the toothpicks. Place the wheel under running water.

4. Tell how the water makes the wheel turn.

Marble Fun Slide

1. Tape together paper towel tubes to make a fun slide.

2. Use books to hold up the tubes.

3. Put a marble at the top, and listen to it race to the bottom. Talk about how it moves.

WRITING

Accordion Book

Make a book that you pull to open and push to close! On each page, write about a push or pull.

READING

What Makes a Magnet? by Franklyn M. Branley
Read more about magnets. Tell two ways people use them.

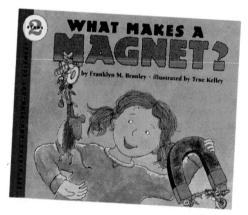

COMPUTER CENTER
Visit *The Learning Site* at
www.harcourtschool.com

References

Science Handbook

Investigating

This plan will help you work like a scientist.

STEP 1 — Ask a question.

Which car will roll the farthest?

STEP 2 — Make a prediction.

I predict this car will win.

STEP 3 — Plan a fair test.

I'll start each car at the same spot.

STEP 4 — Do your test.

I'll measure how far each car rolls.

STEP 5 — Draw a conclusion.

My prediction was correct! This car rolled the farthest.

Investigate More

I wonder if the height of the ramp will make a difference.

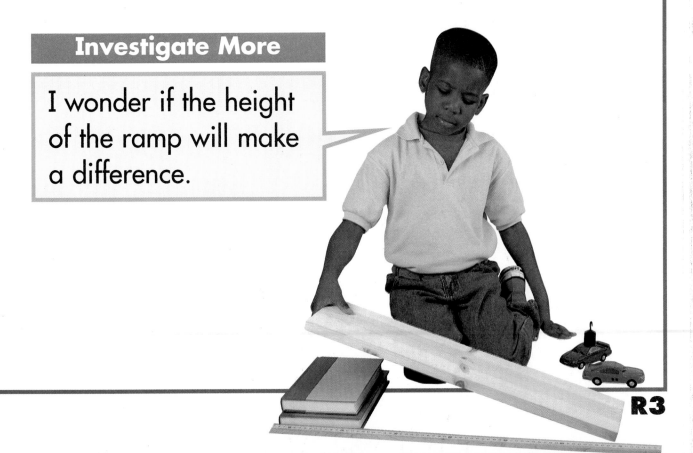

Using Science Tools

Hand Lens

1. Hold the hand lens close to your face
2. Move the object until you see it clearly.

Thermometer

The temperature is 40 degrees.

1. Place the thermometer.
2. Wait two minutes.
3. Find the top of the liquid in the tube.
4. Read the number.

Ruler

1. Put the edge of the ruler at the end of the object.

2. Look at the number at the other end.

3. Read how long the object is.

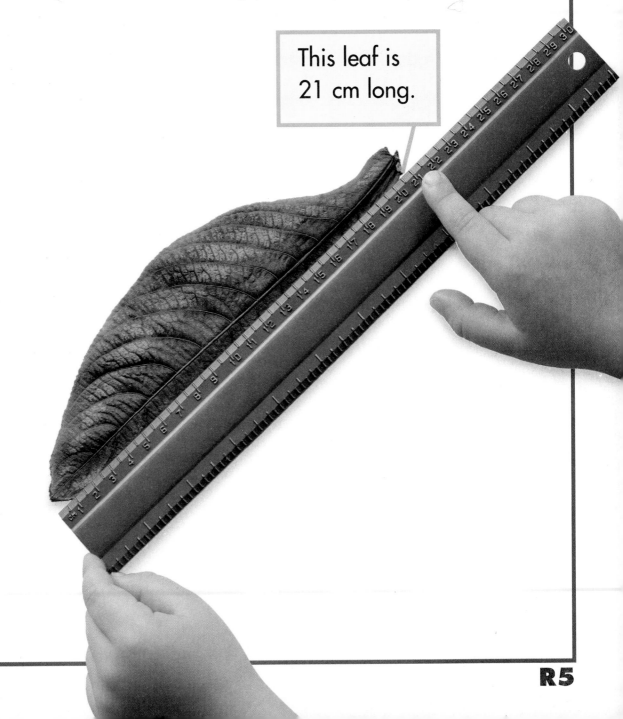

This leaf is 21 cm long.

Measuring Cup

1. Pour the liquid into the cup.
2. Put the cup on a table.
3. Wait until the liquid is still.
4. Look at the level of the liquid.
5. Read how much liquid there is.

There are 150 milliliters of liquid here.

Clock

1. Look at the hour hand.
2. Look at the minute hand.
3. Read the time.

It is 10:00.

Stopwatch

1. To start timing, press START.
2. To stop timing, press STOP.
3. Read how much time has passed.

Now 15 seconds have gone by.

Balance

1. Start with the pans even.
2. Put the object in one pan.
3. Add masses until the pans are even again.
4. Count up the number of masses.

Computer

1. A computer can help you draw.

2. Most computers help you find answers to questions.

3. Many computers help you communicate.

Measurements

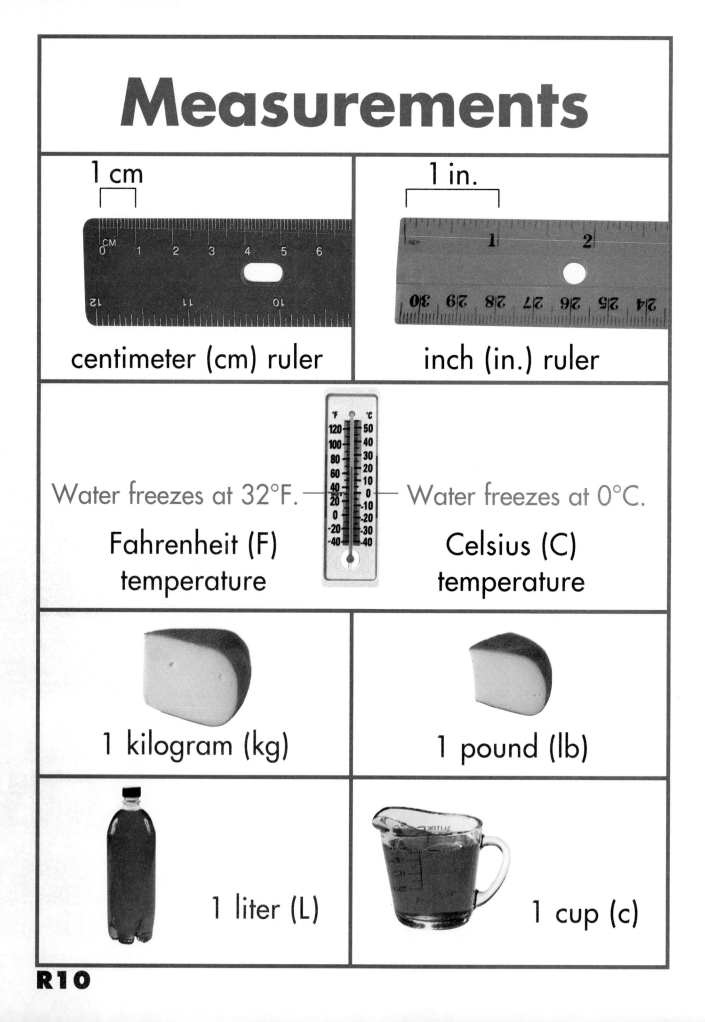

1 cm

centimeter (cm) ruler

1 in.

inch (in.) ruler

Water freezes at 32°F. — Water freezes at 0°C.

Fahrenheit (F)
temperature

Celsius (C)
temperature

1 kilogram (kg)

1 pound (lb)

1 liter (L)

1 cup (c)

Health Handbook

Eyes and Ears

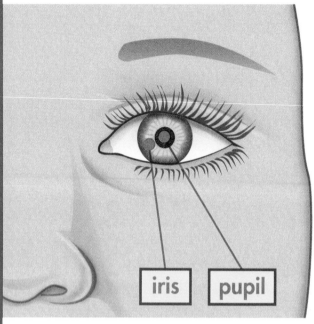

Outside of Eye

Caring for Your Eyes and Ears

- Some bright light can hurt your eyes. Never look at the sun or at very bright lights.
- Never put an object in your ear.

Eyes

When you look at your eyes, you can see a white part, a colored part, and a dark center. The colored part is the iris. The dark center is the pupil.

Inside of Eye

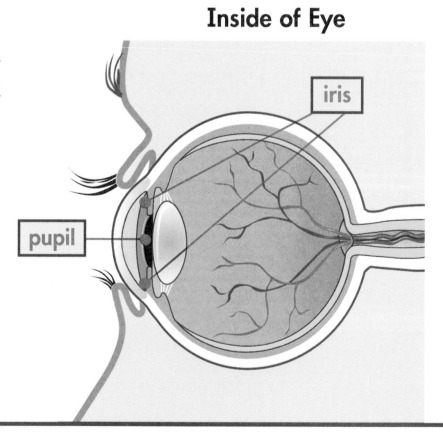

Ear

Your ears let you hear. Most of each ear is inside your head.

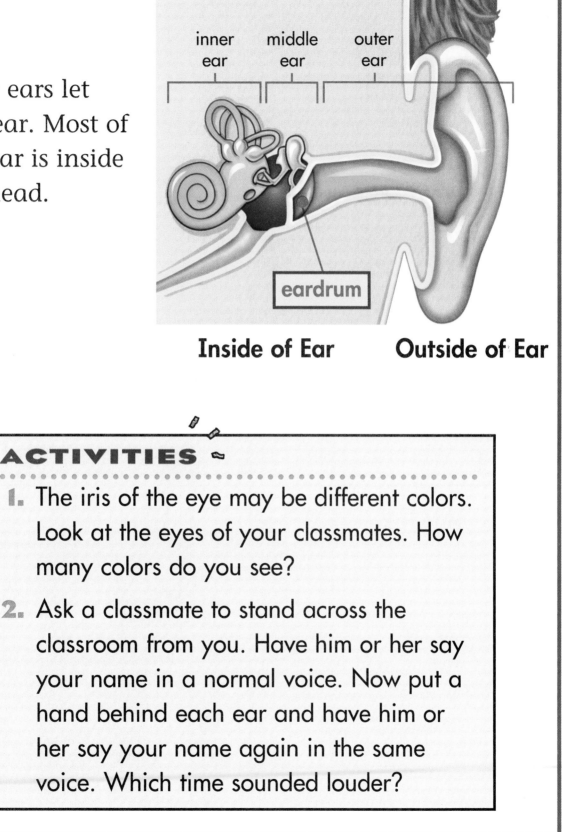

inner ear middle ear outer ear

eardrum

Inside of Ear **Outside of Ear**

ACTIVITIES

1. The iris of the eye may be different colors. Look at the eyes of your classmates. How many colors do you see?

2. Ask a classmate to stand across the classroom from you. Have him or her say your name in a normal voice. Now put a hand behind each ear and have him or her say your name again in the same voice. Which time sounded louder?

The Skeletal System

Inside your body are hard, strong bones. They make up your skeleton. Your skeleton holds you up.

Caring for Your Skeletal System

Protect your head. Wear a helmet when you ride your bike.

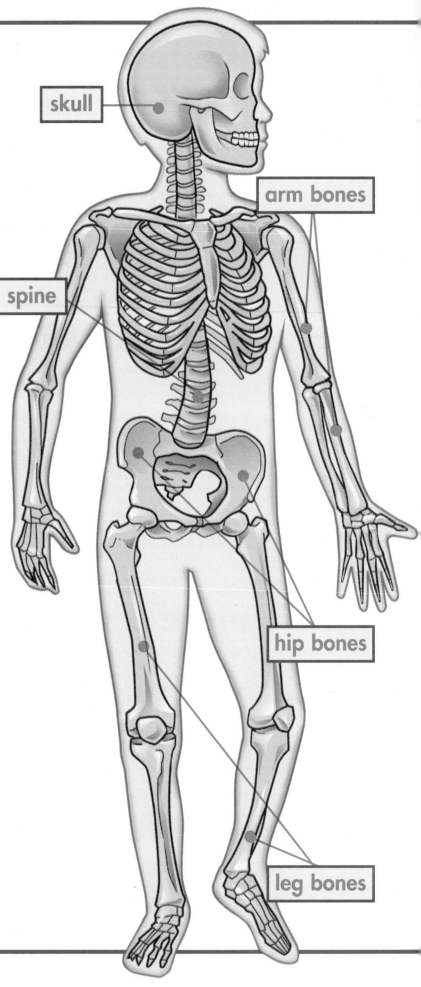

skull

arm bones

spine

hip bones

leg bones

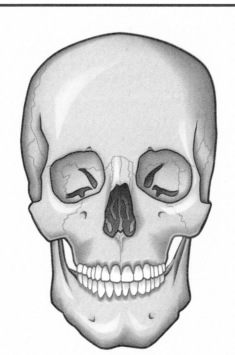

skull

spine

Skull

The bones in your head are called your skull. Your skull protects your brain.

Spine

Your spine, or backbone, is made up of many small bones. Your spine helps you stand up straight.

ACTIVITIES

1. Look at a bike helmet. How is it like your skull?

2. Your foot is about the same length as your arm between your hand and your elbow. Put your foot on your arm and check it out!

The Digestive System

Your digestive system helps your body get energy from the food you eat.

Caring for Your Digestive System

- Brush and floss your teeth every day.
- Don't eat right before you exercise. Your body needs energy to digest food.

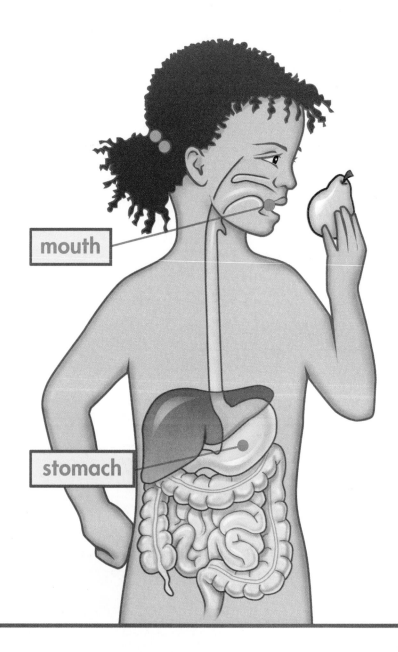

mouth

stomach

Teeth

Some of your teeth tear food and some grind it into small parts.

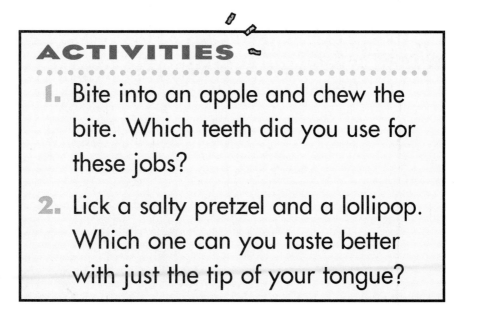

tongue

teeth

Tongue

Your tongue helps you swallow food. It is a strong muscle that also lets you taste.

ACTIVITIES

1. Bite into an apple and chew the bite. Which teeth did you use for these jobs?

2. Lick a salty pretzel and a lollipop. Which one can you taste better with just the tip of your tongue?

The Circulatory System

Blood goes through your body in your circulatory system. Your heart pumps the blood. Your blood vessels carry the blood.

Caring for Your Circulatory System

- Exercise every day to keep your heart strong.
- Keep germs out of your blood. Wash cuts with soap and water. Never touch someone else's blood.

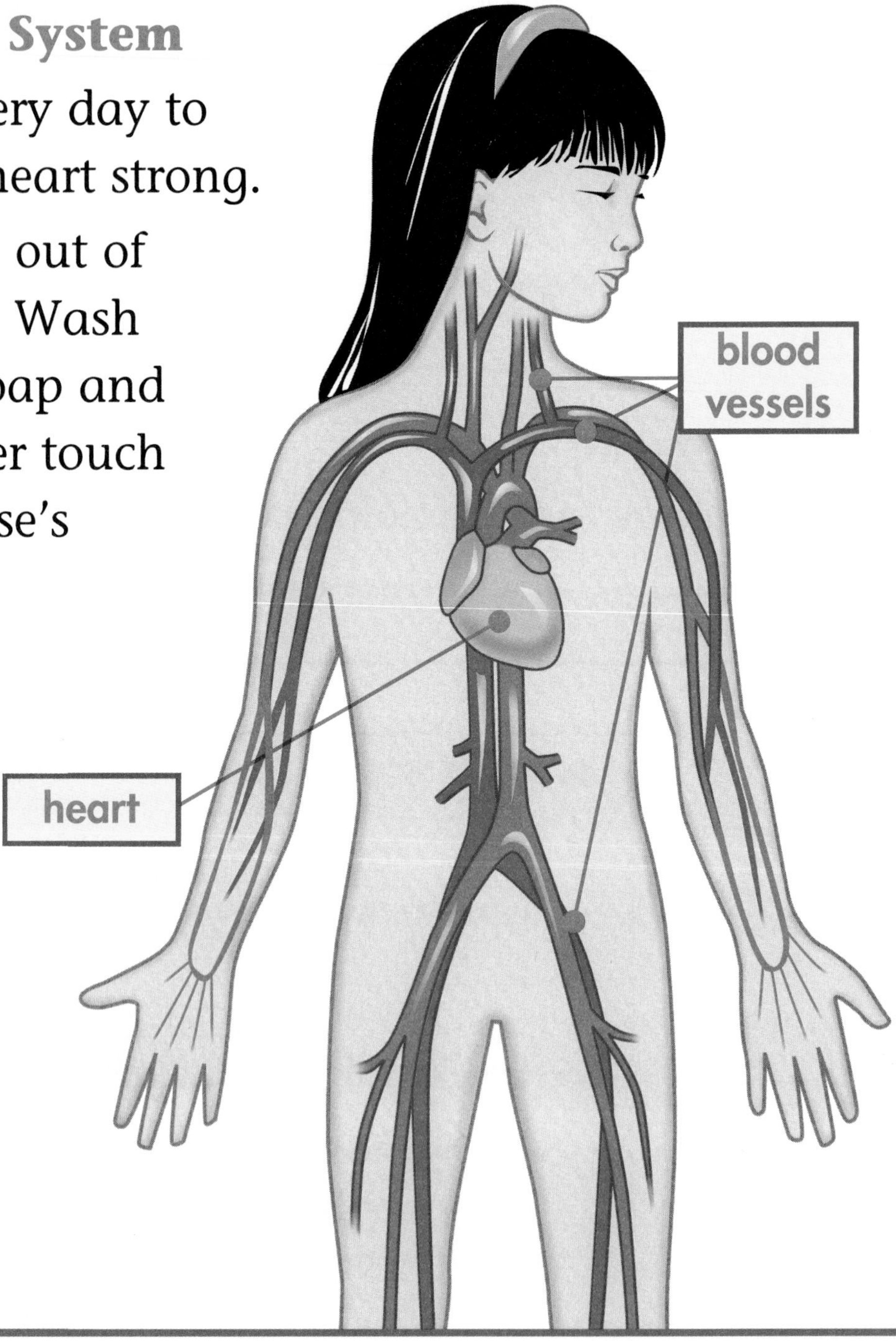

blood vessels

heart

Heart

Your heartbeat is the sound of your heart pumping. Your heart is about the same size as a fist.

fist

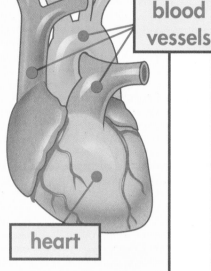

blood vessels

heart

Blood Vessels

Blood vessels are tubes that carry blood through your body.

ACTIVITIES

1. Ask an adult to blow up a hot-dog shaped balloon so that it is not quite full. Squeeze one end. What happens?

2. Put your ear to the middle of a classmate's chest and listen to the heartbeat. Then listen again through a paper cup with the bottom torn out. Which way of listening works better?

The Respiratory System

When you breathe, you are using your respiratory system. Your mouth, your nose, and your lungs are parts of your respiratory system.

Caring for Your Respiratory System

- Never put anything in your nose.

- Exercise makes you breathe harder and is good for your lungs.

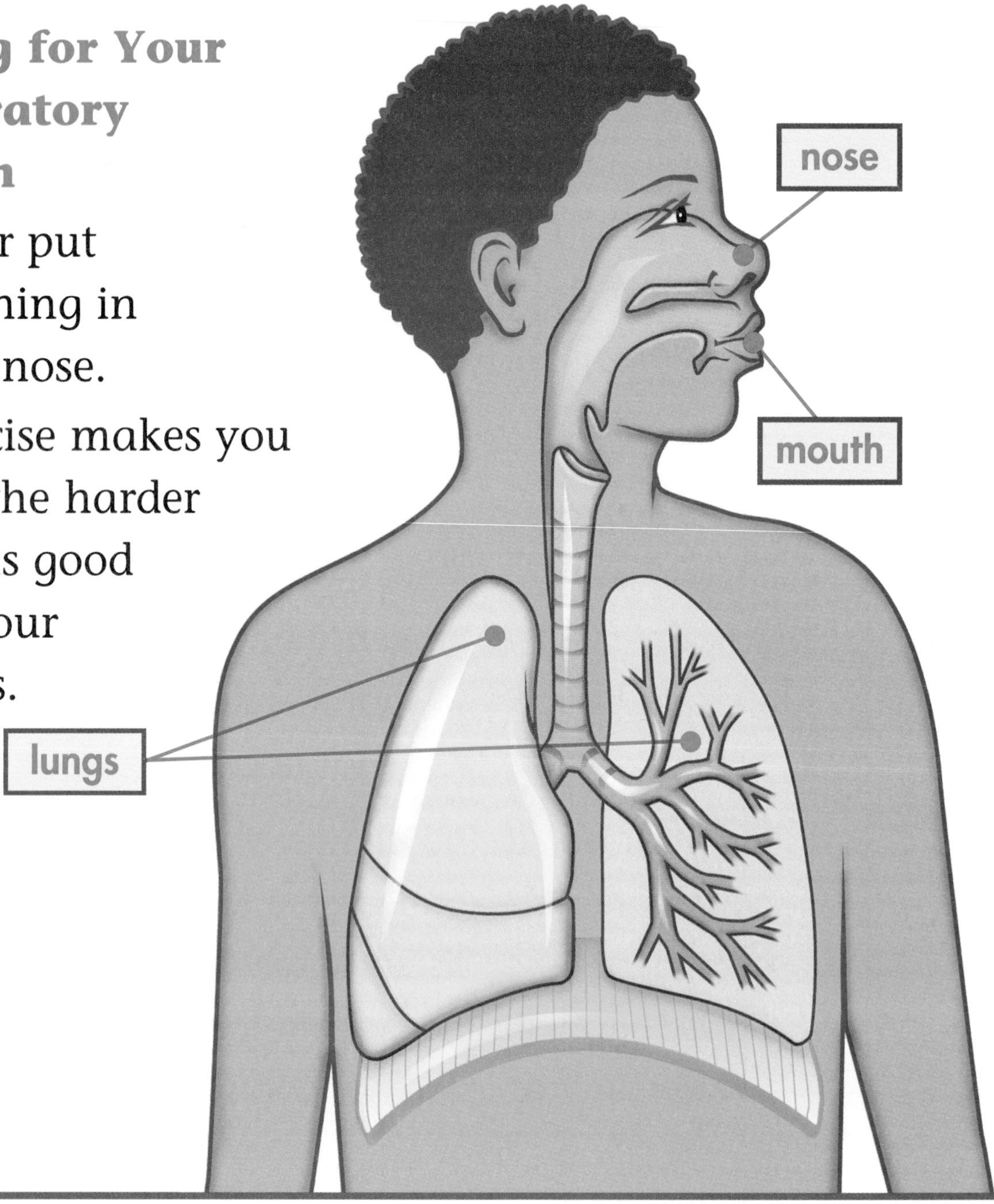

nose

mouth

lungs

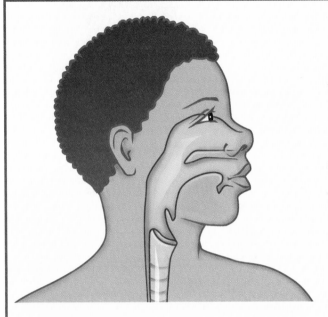

Mouth and Nose

Air goes in and out of your body through your mouth and nose.

Lungs

You have two lungs in your chest. When you breathe in, your lungs fill with air. When you breathe out, air leaves your lungs.

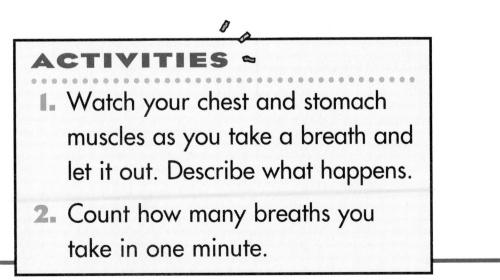

ACTIVITIES

1. Watch your chest and stomach muscles as you take a breath and let it out. Describe what happens.

2. Count how many breaths you take in one minute.

The Muscular System

The muscles in your body help you move.

Caring for Your Muscular System

Warm up your muscles before you play or exercise.

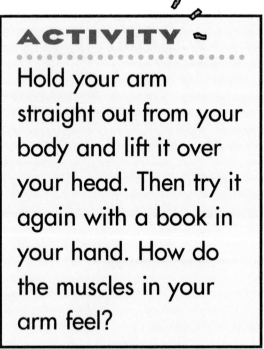

ACTIVITY

Hold your arm straight out from your body and lift it over your head. Then try it again with a book in your hand. How do the muscles in your arm feel?

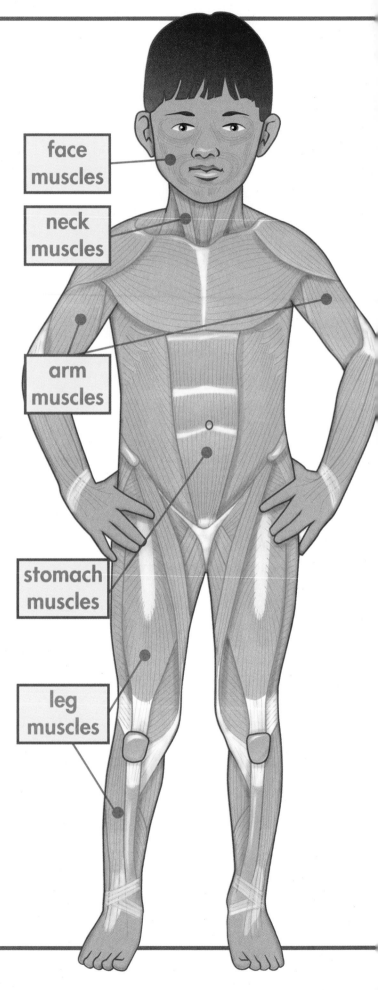

face muscles

neck muscles

arm muscles

stomach muscles

leg muscles

The Nervous System

brain

nerves

Your nervous system keeps your body working and tells you about things around you. Your brain is part of your nervous system.

Caring for Your Nervous System

Get plenty of sleep. Sleeping lets your brain rest.

ACTIVITY

Clap your hands in front of a classmate's face. What happens to his or her eyes?

Staying Safe

Fire Safety

You can stay safe from fires. Follow these safety rules.

- Never play with matches or lighters.
- Be careful around stoves, heaters, fireplaces, and grills.
- Don't use microwaves, irons, or toasters without an adult's help.
- Practice your family's fire safety plan.
- If there is a fire in your home, get out quickly. Drop to the floor and crawl if the room is filled with smoke. If a closed door feels hot, don't open it. Use another exit. Call 911 from outside your home.
- If your clothes catch on fire, use Stop, Drop, and Roll right away to put out the flames.

❶ Stop Don't run or wave your arms.

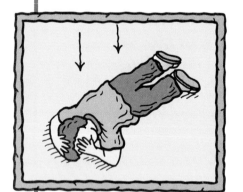

❷ Drop Lie down quickly. Cover your eyes with your hands.

❸ Roll Roll back and forth to put out the fire.

Stranger Danger

NO!

You can stay safe around strangers. Follow these rules.

- Never talk to strangers.
- Never go with a stranger, on foot or in a car.
- If you are home alone, do not open the door. Do not let telephone callers know you are alone.
- Never give your name, address, or phone number to anyone you don't know. (You may give this information to a 911 operator in an emergency.)
- If you are lost or need help, talk to a police officer, a guard, or a store clerk.
- If a stranger bothers you, use the Stranger Danger rules to stay safe.

❶ **Say no!** Yell if you need to. You do not have to be polite to strangers.

❷ **Get away.** Walk fast or run in the opposite direction. Go toward people who can help you.

❸ **Tell someone.** Tell a trusted adult, such as a family member, a teacher, or a police officer. Do not keep secrets about strangers.

R25

Staying Safe
A Safe Bike

To ride your bike safely, you need to start with a safe bike. A safe bike is the right size for you. When you sit on your bike with the pedal in the lowest position, you should be able to rest your heel on the pedal.

After checking the size of your bike, check to see that it has the right safety equipment. Your bike should have everything shown below.

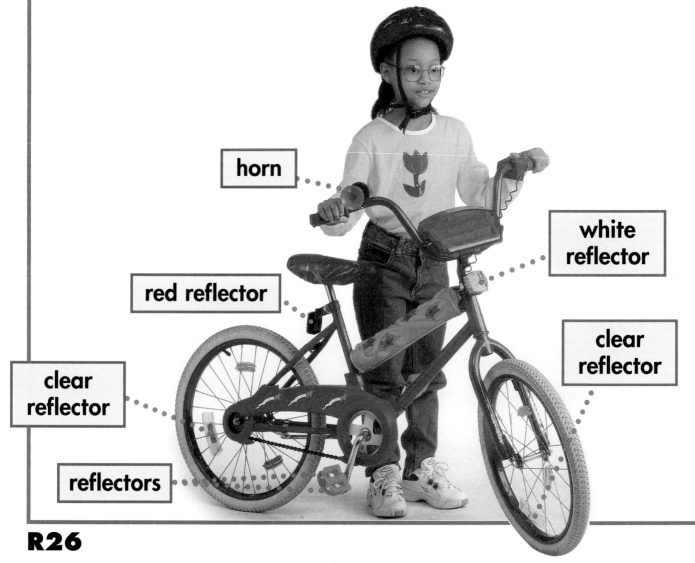

horn

white reflector

red reflector

clear reflector

clear reflector

reflectors

Your Bike Helmet

◀ Always wear a bike helmet. Wear your helmet flat on your head. Be sure it is strapped tightly. If your helmet gets bumped in a fall, replace it right away, even if it doesn't look damaged.

Safety on the Road

- Check your bike for safety every time you ride it.
- Ride in single file. Ride in the same direction as traffic.
- Stop, look, listen, and think when you enter a street or cross a driveway.
- Walk your bike across an intersection.
- Obey all traffic signs and signals.
- Don't ride at night without an adult. Wear light-colored clothing and use lights and reflectors for night riding.

GLOSSARY

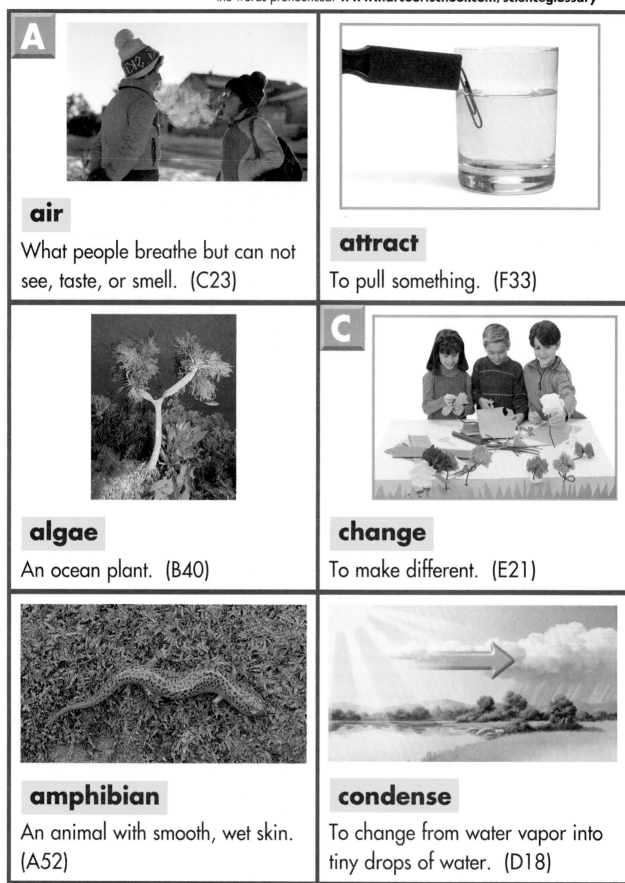

A

air
What people breathe but can not see, taste, or smell. (C23)

attract
To pull something. (F33)

algae
An ocean plant. (B40)

C

change
To make different. (E21)

amphibian
An animal with smooth, wet skin. (A52)

condense
To change from water vapor into tiny drops of water. (D18)

D

desert

A dry place. (B31)

E

enrich

To make better. (B12)

evaporate

To change from water into water vapor. (D18)

F

fall

The season that follows summer. (D35)

float

To stay on top of a liquid. (E13)

flowers

The part of a plant that makes seeds. (A27)

force

A push or a pull. (F5)

friction

A force that makes it harder to move things. (F20)

forest

A place where many trees grow. (B27)

G

gas

Matter that does not have a shape of its own, such as air. (E17)

fresh water

Water that is not salty. (C27)

gills

Body part that helps a fish take air from water. (A47)

H

hatch

To break out of an egg. (A60)

heat

What is given off by fire or by the sun. (E35)

I

insect

An animal that has three body parts and six legs. (A55)

L

lake

A body of water with land all around it. (C28)

larva

A caterpillar. (A66)

leaves

The plant part that makes food for the plant. (A26)

liquid

Matter that flows to take the shape of its container. (E9)

magnetic force

The pulling force of a magnet. (F43)

living

Need food, water, and air to live and grow. (A11)

magnetize

To give magnetic force to something a magnet attracts. (F47)

M

magnet

A piece of iron that pulls things made of iron. (F33)

mammal

An animal that has hair or fur and feeds its young milk. (A50)

matter

Everything around you. (E5)

motion

Movement from one place to another. (F13)

mechanic

A person who can fix a broken car part or put in a new one. (E27)

N

nonliving

Does not need food, water, and air and does not grow. (A11)

melt

To change from a solid to a liquid. (E40)

O

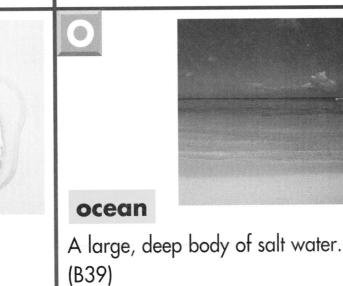

ocean

A large, deep body of salt water. (B39)

poles

The places where the pulling force of a magnet is strongest. (F39)

product

Something that people make from other things. (B16)

pollen

The powder in flowers that helps flowers make seeds. (B13)

pull

To tug something closer. (F5)

prism

A clear object that breaks light into its colors. (E45)

pupa

A hard covering over a caterpillar. (A67)

push

To press something away. (F5)

refract

To bend or change the direction of light. (E49)

R

rain forest

A forest that is wet all year. (B35)

repel

To push away. (F40)

reflect

To bounce back light. (E48)

reptile

An animal with rough, dry skin. (A52)

river

A body of moving water that is larger than a stream. (C28)

salt water

Water that has salt in it. (C31)

rock

A hard, nonliving thing that comes from the Earth. (C5)

sand

Tiny, broken pieces of rock. (C6)

roots

A plant part that holds plants in the soil and takes in water. (A24)

season

One of four times of the year—fall, winter, spring, and summer. (D27)

seed

What most plants grow from. (A29)

shelter

A place where an animal can be safe. (B8)

seed coat

Covering a seed may have. (A29)

sink

To drop to the bottom of a liquid. (E13)

senses

Touch, sight, smell, hearing, and taste. (A5)

soil

The part of Earth's surface that is made of tiny rocks and bits of dead plants and animals. (C9)

solid

Matter that keeps its shape. (E6)

stream

A body of moving water smaller than a river. (C28)

spring

The season that follows winter. (D27)

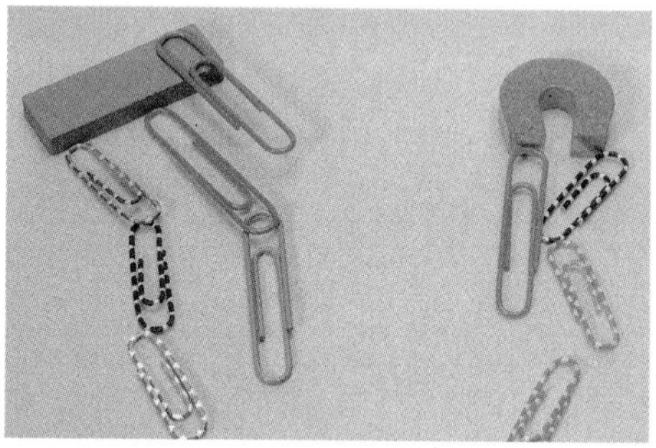

strength

How strong something is, such as a magnet's pull. (F37)

stem

Plant part that helps hold up the plant and moves water to the leaves. (A25)

summer

The season that follows spring. (D31)

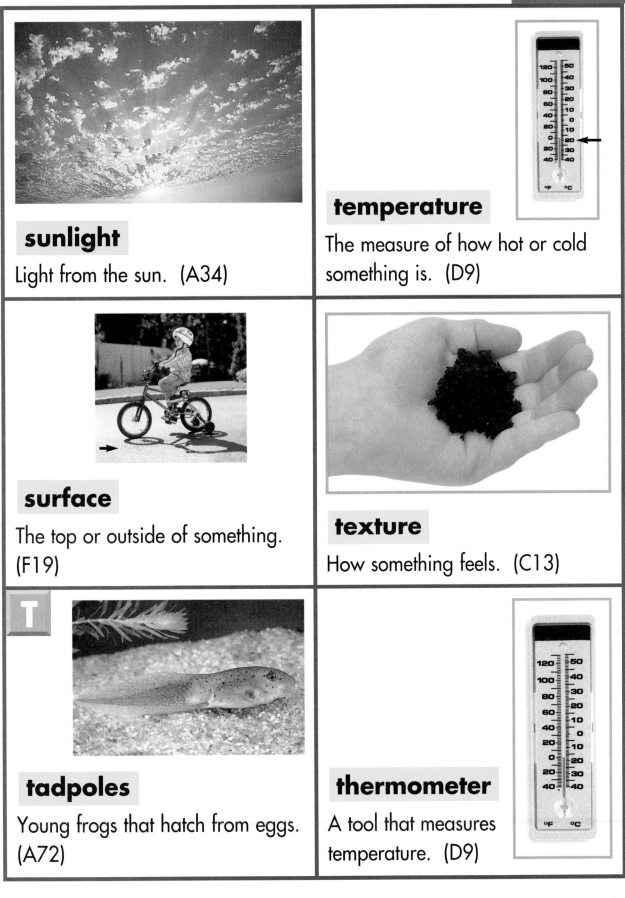

sunlight

Light from the sun. (A34)

temperature

The measure of how hot or cold something is. (D9)

surface

The top or outside of something. (F19)

texture

How something feels. (C13)

T

tadpoles

Young frogs that hatch from eggs. (A72)

thermometer

A tool that measures temperature. (D9)

R39

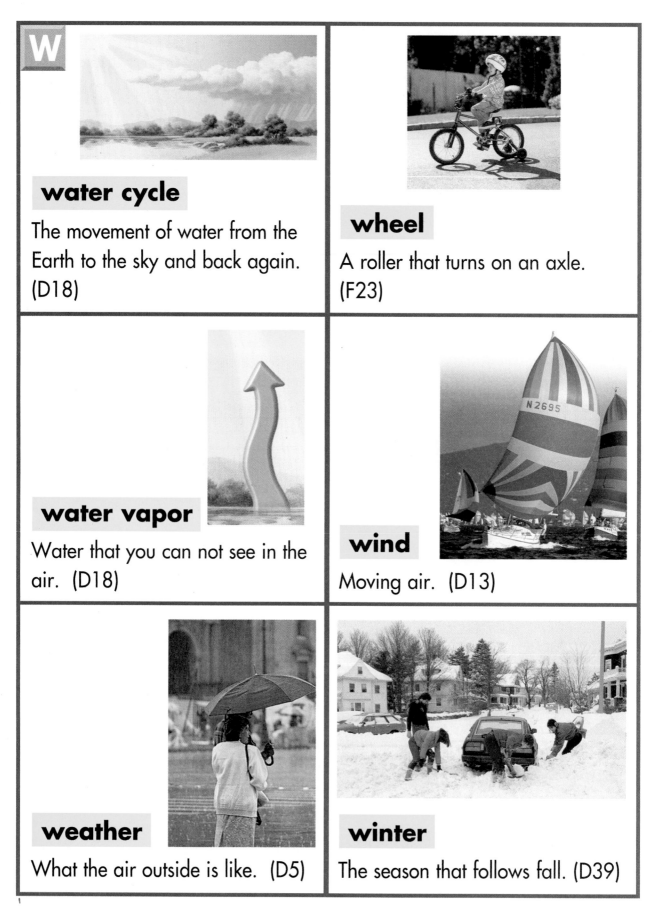

water cycle

The movement of water from the Earth to the sky and back again. (D18)

wheel

A roller that turns on an axle. (F23)

water vapor

Water that you can not see in the air. (D18)

wind

Moving air. (D13)

weather

What the air outside is like. (D5)

winter

The season that follows fall. (D39)

Z

zigzag

With sharp turns back and forth.
(F10)

General Instructions

Before Starting

As you read this book, it is helpful to understand its basic structure. Each chapter describes a different technique in card creation. The general direction for the techniques is explained in the opening section of each chapter, but not repeated for each example. The specific instructions, materials, and tools needed are listed with each card to make replication of each card quick and easy. Remember the following:

1. Read all General Instructions. Gather all General Materials & Tools along with specific materials and tools for the project.

2. Copy or trace and transfer specific patterns from pages 103–125 onto appropriate card stock or cover stock. Enlarge cards and designs as needed or specified.

3. Cut out cards and designs with craft scissors.

4. Apply glue or desired adhesive to back of designs.

5. Refer to individual project photographs as guidelines for placement of photograph, designs, and stickers.

It is entirely possible to "mix and match" elements from one card to another or to substitute elements more personal to you and the card recipient. Patterns in the back of the book can be enlarged or reduced as desired.

Personalized messages placed on the card can be created with computer-generated fonts and press-on letters, or handwritten with decorative pens. Embellish designs as desired. Details can also be added with stickers, colored pens, and colored pencils.

General Materials & Tools

The following materials and tools are needed to create all the greeting cards in this book. These materials and tools are not listed with the individual projects.

Craft scissors

Glue stick or desired adhesive

Ruler

Tracing paper or photocopy machine for patterns on pages 103–125

Love on page 59.

5

Adhesives

- **Adhesive Foam Dots** are self-adhesive foam dots about ¼" thick. The adhesive is on both sides. They are used to add dimension to greeting cards. Apply foam dots on the back of photographs and designs to make them literally lift off the card.

- **Double-sided Tape** is a handy alternative to mounting adhesive sheets. It is available in rolls, like regular clear tape, and is applied directly on the back of the cutout or photograph. There are several types of double-sided tape. Some double-sided tape has a peel-off shield to prevent one side from being exposed to dust particles or lint.

- **Foam Tape** is two-sided self-adhesive foam that works the same as the foam dot, but is presented in a roll. Cut segments to the desired size and apply on the back of designs to lift elements off the card.

- **Glue Sticks** are inexpensive and easy to use. Remove the cap, apply the glue directly on the design and adhere the design onto the greeting card.

- **Mounting Adhesive Sheets** are available in 8½" x 11" sheets. Cut a piece of mounting adhesive approximately the same size as the cut-out pattern. Adhere one side of the mounting adhesive onto the back of the

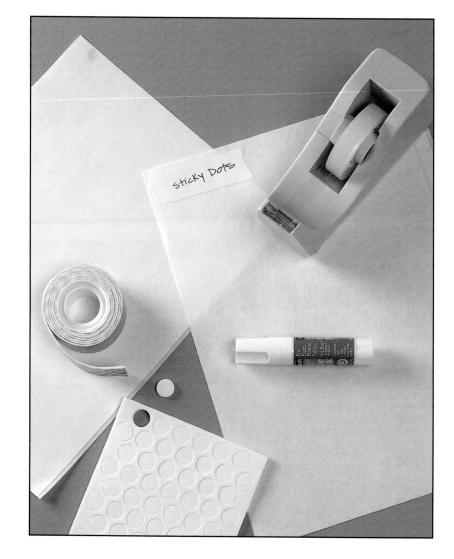

paper and cut out the design. For ease and convenience, a mounting adhesive sheet may be mounted onto an entire sheet of paper before cutting.

- **Sticky Dots** are a sheet of tiny dots that lift off onto the design. Peel off protective liner and place the design onto the sticky dots. Rub your fingers over the shape to transfer the adhesive to the design. Peel liner off and place design.

- **The Xyron™ Machine** can be used to apply an adhesive on the back of virtually any material. Roll full sheets of paper through the Xyron Machine to apply adhesive. Peel the adhesive backing from the design and place on the greeting card.

Craft Punches

Craft punches generally provide a smaller version of a design for those times when tiny decorations are needed on the greeting card. Both positive and negative shapes may be used. They are available at craft stores and come in a variety of styles, shapes, and sizes.

- **Border Punches** are another type of craft punch. The design is presented in a horizontal strip. When cut from clear plastic, border punches provide an effective tool for making a stencil.

- **Corner Punches** are used for rounding corners of greeting cards and photographs. Some corner rounders punch a decorative element in the corner of the card at the same time.

- **Hand-held Craft Punches** resemble the traditional hand-held hole punch but have a decorative shape instead of a plain round hole.

- **Thumb Punches** use the palm of the hand or the thumb to apply pressure for cutting. Thumb punches are available in small, large, jumbo, and in a wide variety of designs.

A hand-held craft punch was used to create the tiny hearts surrounding the window of this Dangle Card. See page 93.

7

Patterns

Each greeting card described in this book comes with its own pattern(s) that can be found on pages 103–125. Do not cut out the patterns from this book. Trace patterns onto tracing paper or photocopy, then cut out patterns. Transfer patterns onto desired card stock or cover stock. Cut out designs.

Patterns can also be photocopied at a copy center directly onto card stock. All patterns are actual size unless otherwise noted. Many patterns include perforated lines to use as guidelines for creasing or for embellishing in contrasting colors. Solid lines are used as guidelines for cutting or making slits.

If you do not wish to use the patterns in this book, die-cuts are an option. A list of Ellison dies is provided on page 126, which corresponds with the patterns on pages 103–125.

Die-cuts

Die-cuts are precut shapes of paper or lightweight card stock. Most of the patterns provided in this book are available in die-cuts. They are made by putting a die into a special press called a die-cutting machine, along with the desired paper, card stock, or clear page protector.

They are one of the easiest ways to decorate a greeting card and may be used to replace hand-cut designs. Adhere die-cuts onto cards, using a glue stick, or mount onto the cards with mounting adhesive sheets. It is easiest to mount adhesive to paper first, then cut in a die-cutting machine. Die-cuts are available at most craft stores and are sold individually or in theme packets. All of the card formats are also die-cuts.

Die-cutting machines are available for use in many craft stores. Stores generally do not charge to use the machines, if you purchase the paper or card stock from the store. Also, look for them in stationery stores, fine-art stores, photograph shops, and stores that sell rubber stamps.

Die-cutting machines allow for creative control when cutting shapes and letters for greeting cards. Select your own paper colors and designs for the die-cuts. Cut as many of each design or letter as needed for your greeting cards. Cut a wide assortment of products, such as maps, theater programs, sheet music, comic strips, wallpaper, self-adhesive paper, etc. You can even cut rubber for rubber stamps of your own design. Die-cutting machines will cut anything scissors will cut; fabric, felt, thin plastic, and other decorative elements can be added to your greetings cards. Die-cutting machines can also be used to emboss elegant features on cards.

Embellishments

Transform a simple design into a finely detailed design. See photograph. Embellishing can be as simple as cutting the stem off of a green apple and placing it on a red apple, or placing a gold fish with pierced holes over a green fish.

Embellish a design by adding multiple layers of patterned or contrasting paper for more detail.

Embellish a design by cutting one design from multiple colors. Trim away the unwanted sections and layer on top of base shape.

Lettering and Pens

Lettering can be computer-generated, handwritten, or pressed on using stickers or press-on letters.

- **Black Felt-tipped Pens** are available in varying sized tips and are perfect for drawing line borders on cards and handwriting a message.

- **Colored Felt-tipped Pens** are great for hand-coloring details on a card.

- **Gel Roller Pens** are similar to paint pens but create a finer line. The color is not as saturated, but is easier to work with. Also, there are no problems with paint clumping or skipping.

- **Paint Pens** make it easy to put any color print on top of any color material. The product in the pen is paint and makes a fairly thick line.

Papers

Choices for paper have never been greater. From handmade paper, to paper for scrapbooking, to colorful stationery, paper is available in an endless variety of colors, patterns, textures, and weights. Use these varieties to help create themes and moods.

- **Cover Stock** and **Card Stock** are more rigid than paper, making excellent choices for cards and card covers.

- **Legal Size Papers** are available at office supplies stores. They measure 8" x 14".

- **Page Protectors** are easily cut into various envelope sizes for a special see-through card effect.

- **Plain-colored Papers** are available in a wide range of weights. In most cases, the bulk of the card will be cut from plain and contrasting-colored card stock, with patterned or textured paper for accent pieces.

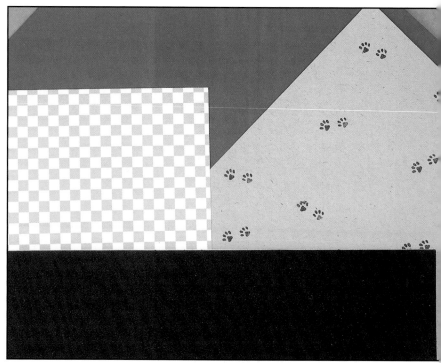

- **Patterned Papers**, such as stationery or wrapping paper, are medium- to lightweight. They add contrast or complement other decorative elements on the card.

- **Vellum Paper** adds a unique feature to cards. The vellum allows elements on the card to be visible through a filmy layer of paper. Print or photocopy directly onto its surface for a very special effect.

Stickers

Stickers add a decorative element to greeting cards. Use elegant stickers to decorate a wedding or anniversary card and whimsical designs for a child's birthday party invitation.

- **Border stickers** are created specifically for use as borders called design lines.

- **Stickers** are available in a wide variety of styles, covering a large assortment of themes.

Paper Cutters, Scissors, and Trimmers

Many craft stores have heavy-duty paper cutters for your use. Some are available with different blades or decorative edges.

- **Decorative-edged Scissors** are used for enhancing the edges and corners of paper motifs, mats, photographs, and card edges. There is a wide variety of edge patterns from simple scallops to lacy Victorian.

- **Decorative Corner Edgers** create a patterned edge for each corner of the card. The pattern can be continued down the four sides of the card, or used solely as a corner design.

- **Paper Trimmers and Scissors** are used for cutting paper, light plastic, and other materials. Select a pair with comfortable handles to make card projects easier. A small pair helps to trim with better control.

Rubber Stamps

Rubber stamps provide another option for decorating greeting cards. They are easy to use and come in a wide variety of shapes and sizes, making it easy to find stamps to coordinate with the theme of a card. Decorate the image with felt-tipped pens after stamping, or emboss them with embossing powder and powder heating tools. It is also possible to make your own patterned paper, using tiny rubber stamps. Ink pads can be used with any traditional rubber stamp and come in every color of the rainbow. There are many stamps available that decoratively print the lines of information for party and shower invitations or birth announcements.

11

Creative Greeting Cards

A distinctive envelope arrives in the mail among bills, junk mail, and catalogs. The bulk of the mail is discarded while the envelope gathers all of your attention. Why is that? You know that inside is a special offering selected or created with one person in mind . . . you! There is no doubt that a unique card creates a vibrant impression, stronger and more lasting than any phone call, fax, or e-mail.

There are many reasons for creating a special card for a special friend. A handmade card allows for the message to fit the person or

occasion in a way that a store-bought card cannot. The card can reflect the personality of the card maker as well as the recipient.

Creating your own cards, makes good sense financially. Store-bought cards can be expensive. Making a card by hand is a great way to save a little money. It also provides an opportunity to use remnants from around the house—everything from wrapping paper to string, from buttons to wallpaper, and more.

The therapeutic value of card creation is priceless. A creative outlet for ideas can be as relaxing as a day at the beach.

Whether you are just beginning your card-making skills or are already a veteran card maker, you will find the creation of these quick and easy. Don't be misled into thinking that these cards are difficult to make. Whether working with die-cut shapes or the patterns provided in the back of the book, the basic card design is complete with perforation lines and cutouts, making replication easier than you might think. Included are cards for all occasions: Christmas, Hanukkah, birthdays, Easter, Halloween, valentines, Mother's Day, Father's Day, wedding, and just to say hello. In addition, you will find birth announcements, party invitations, and thank you cards. Each card is designed to convey a message in a unique and special way.

I hope the cards in this book help to jump-start your creativity and inspire you to create your own clever cards.

Thank You on page 55.

Greeting Card Tips

▪ Make certain to start with the envelope. Whether your card is being sent through the mail or left under a pillow, the presentation is more special if the card is housed in an envelope. Whether the envelope is purchased or handmade, select it first and create your card to fit.

▪ Remember the value of a black or white background for your cards. There is nothing that will make bright colors pop like basic black or white.

▪ Be aware that substitution is always possible. Replace primary colors with pastels. Substitute patterned card stock for plain card stock. Trade star stickers for hearts. Make each project as personal as possible by selecting the products, styles, and themes that are personal favorites of the card maker or the card recipient.

▪ When planning your card composition, keep in mind that it is good to have an element that slightly overlaps another element. Both elements should be clearly visible, but a slight overlap helps to keep the composition from looking too rigid or too symmetrical.

▪ Know when to stop. Usually the best design is deceivingly simple and clean. Too much activity in the design will only be confusing and isn't as appealing as a sharp clean look.

▪ Remember the third dimension. Cards don't have to be limited to a flat surface. Elements can pop up or hang down for a very special effect.

What's Up? on page 36.

▪ Remember you have the perfect tool right in your photograph album to personalize many cards. Birth announcements, graduation, and annual Christmas cards are only enhanced by the inclusion of a photograph. Instead of tucking the photograph in the envelope, build the photograph into the design of the card. Copy favorite photographs and save your valuable originals. Color copy machines and duplicate photograph machines are readily available and make this a simple task.

▪ Multiple mats are a quick and easy way to add bright color and detail to any card. A thin line or border drawn with a pen and ruler can enhance a multiple mat.

▪ Organize supplies and keep them handy, allowing you to grab a few minutes here and there to work on cards.

▪ Try to set aside a little time on a consistent basis for card creation. If a given time is scheduled, you are more likely to get to it.

▪ Jot down notes for future cards and store them with your supplies. Note which cards you have sent special friends to avoid sending a similar card in the future.

Accordion Cards

Accordion Cards involve the folding of paper into accordion pleats. The pleats can vary in number and size and can be presented horizontally or vertically. The pleats fold up fairly flat, but will spread when opened to reveal several layers of design in a card.

Accordion Cards are created with either an Accordion Card Pattern on page 104, Accordion Fold #1 Pattern on page 103, or Accordion Fold #2 Pattern on page 105. (Accordion Card is on the left and Accordion Fold #1 is on the right in the photograph above.)

The Accordion Card or the Accordion Fold #1 is attached onto front and back card covers. See photograph at left. Accordion Fold #2 is not shown.

Hugs & Kisses

Instructions

Refer to General Instructions on pages 5–13.

1. Enlarge Accordion Fold #2 Pattern 38%. Transfer pattern onto white cover stock.

2. Cut out card.

3. Cut cover ⅛" larger than card all around from black cover stock. Center and adhere card onto cover.

4. Crease card on perforation lines, creating pleats.

5. Cut Xs and Os as desired from assorted colored card stock, varying sizes.

6. Adhere Xs and Os onto inside back of card and pleats, allowing portion of each letter to extend over edges of pleats.

7. Place letters on left-hand side of card for Hugs & Kisses.

8. Cut strip from red cover stock to fit horizontally inside card. Note: The size of strip will be determined by length of message.

9. Using black pen and ruler, draw pen lines onto strip. Write desired message on strip.

10. Adhere strip onto inside of card.

Materials & Tools

Black felt-tipped pen

Card stock: assorted colors; assorted patterns

Cover stock: black; red; white

Pattern: Accordion Fold #2 (pg. 105)

Press-on letters for Hugs & Kisses: ¼"

Ruler

Zing Went the Strings of My Heart

Instructions

Refer to General Instructions on pages 5–13.

1. Enlarge Accordion Fold #2 Pattern 38%. Transfer pattern onto white cover stock.

2. Transfer Primitive Heart Pattern onto patterned card stock. Repeat. Repeat two times with red card stock.

3. Cut out card and designs. Using craft knife, cut two vertical slits into each heart.

4. Weave thread through slits in hearts.

5. Cut cover ¼" larger than card all around from black cover stock. Center and adhere card onto cover.

6. Cut thin strip from black card stock to fit horizontally inside bottom of card.

7. Using silver pen, write desired message on black strip. Adhere strip onto card.

8. Crease card and cover on perforation lines, creating pleats.

9. Adhere hearts onto each panel, overlapping third and fourth heart. See photograph. Place foam dots on back of third heart.

10. Pull thread to allow play when pleats are closed and opened. Trim excess thread.

11. Using black pen, complete message. See photograph.

Materials & Tools

Adhesive foam dots

Black thread

Card stock: black; red; red/white patterned

Cover stock: black; white

Craft knife

Patterns: Accordion Fold #2 (pg. 105); Primitive Heart (pg. 103)

Pen: black felt-tipped; silver metallic

Joy to the World

Instructions

Refer to General Instructions on pages 5–13.

1. Enlarge Accordion Fold #2 Pattern 38%. Transfer pattern onto cover stock.

2. Transfer Hook Pattern onto black card stock. Repeat three times.

3. Transfer Christmas Ornament #1B Pattern onto blue card stock. Repeat three times with assorted colored card stock.

4. Cut out card and designs. Using craft knife, cut out highlights for ornaments. See photograph. Adhere a piece of contrasting colored card stock onto back of highlight on back of ornaments.

5. Crease card on perforation lines.

6. Cut 4½" x 6" rectangle from cover stock. Adhere to last panel.

7. Insert hooks through ornaments.

8. Draw continents on green card stock and cut out. Adhere onto blue ornament. Adhere ornament onto last panel of card.

9. Using red pen, write desired message on last panel inside of card around ornament.

Materials & Tools

Card stock: assorted colors; black; blue; green

Cover stock: white

Craft knife

Patterns: Accordion Fold #2 (pg. 105); Christmas Ornament #1B (pg. 103); Hook (pg. 103)

Red fine-point felt-tipped pen

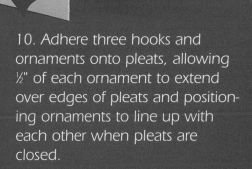

10. Adhere three hooks and ornaments onto pleats, allowing ½" of each ornament to extend over edges of pleats and positioning ornaments to line up with each other when pleats are closed.

For Whom the Bell Jingles

Materials & Tools

Black felt-tipped pen

Christmas floral sticker

Cover stock: cream; green; red

Double-sided tape

Green ribbon: ⅛"-wide

Jingle bells: small (2); med.

Patterns: Accordion Fold with Slits (pg. 105); Large Accordion Card (pg. 105)

Ruler

Instructions

Refer to General Instructions on pages 5–13.

1. Enlarge Large Accordion Card Pattern 35%. Enlarge Accordion Fold with Slits Pattern 52%.

2. Transfer Large Accordion Card Pattern onto cream cover stock. Cut out card.

3. Cut out 3"-wide rectangle from center of card. Crease card on perforation lines, creating pleats.

4. Transfer Accordion Fold with Slits Pattern onto red cover stock. Cut out Accordion Fold with Slits. Cut slits in fold as shown on pattern. Crease fold on perforation lines, creating pleats.

5. Position red fold in cream card, using slits. See photograph at right.

6. Cut three pieces of ribbon into desired lengths to hang jingle bells from card. Thread one end of ribbon through hook on each jingle bell. Tape ribbon ends onto back of card in pleats.

7. Cut two 4" x 6½" covers from green cover stock for front and back.

8. Adhere one end of card ¼" in from edge of front cover. Repeat for remaining end of card and back cover.

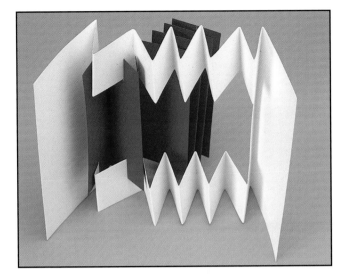

9. Cut two 2¾" x 5½" rectangles from red card stock.

10. Using black pen, write desired message on rectangles. Center and adhere rectangles onto front and back inside of card. See photograph at right.

11. Cut 3" x 5" rectangle from cream cover stock to decorate front cover.

12. Using black pen and ruler, create border around rectangle. Write desired message on rectangle.

13. Center and adhere rectangle onto front of cover. Place floral sticker over top edge of cream rectangle.

New Year's Card

Materials & Tools

Adhesive foam dots

Black paper

Card stock: black; blue; gold; gold metallic; green; purple; red

Computer

Cover stock: white, 35" x 6½"

Gold metallic pen

Patterns: Christmas Ornament #2A (pg. 104); Current Year (pg. 103); Holly Leaves (pg. 104); Primitive Star (pg. 104); Tiny Christmas Light (pg. 104); Upcoming Year (pg. 103)

Red jingle bell

Ruler

Stickers: border; floral; heart; lips; star

Thumb punch: mini Christmas tree

White thread

Instructions

Refer to General Instructions on pages 5–13.

Note: Designs are all cut in pairs.

1. Fold white cover stock into seven equal panels. See photograph. Note: Each panel measures 5"x 6½".

2. Using craft knife, cut out 2¾" square from center of each panel.

3. Transfer Christmas Ornament #2A Pattern onto gold card stock. Repeat. Cut two.

4. Transfer Holly Leaves Pattern, and Current Year onto green card stock. Cut two of each.

5. Transfer Primitive Star Pattern onto red card stock. Cut two.

6. Transfer Tiny Christmas Light Pattern onto purple card stock. Cut two. Repeat with blue card stock. Cut two.

7. Transfer Upcoming Year Pattern onto purple card stock. Cut two. Repeat with metallic card stock. Cut one.

8. Using thumb punch, punch out four trees.

9. Cut seven pieces of thread into desired lengths to hang designs from card. Thread one end of thread through hook on jingle bell. Sandwich double thread vertically between two ornament cutouts.

10. Sandwich one end of thread vertically between each set of cutouts except metallic design. Match and adhere designs together. Using various stickers, hang thread from center front of panels, leaving designs to dangle freely. See photograph on facing page.

11. Print corresponding messages in reverse type with borders to appear under each window. See Card's Mes-sage below. Note:

Black card stock and white felt-tipped pen can be used if a computer is not available or desired. Cut messages into equal-sized strips.

12. Adhere one strip ¼" below each window.

13. Cut 12" x 4" rectangle from red card stock for slider.

14. Wrap slider around card, overlapping short ends in back. Adhere ends.

15. Cut 2½" x 3½" rectangle from black card stock. Center and adhere metallic design onto rectangle as desired.

16. Place two foam dots on back of rectangle. Place rectangle on front of slider as desired.

17. Using gold pen and ruler, create border around outside of rectangle.

Card's Message:

Kiss the Century Good-Bye (first panel)

It's Been Delightful (second panel)

Time for a Shiny New Beginning (third panel)

Think Tree Mendous Thoughts (fourth panel)

Ring in the New Century (fifth panel)

And Have a Happy Holly Day (sixth panel)

Enjoy . . . Burma Shave (seventh panel)

Thought I'd Drop You a Line

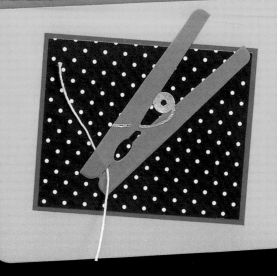

Just Thought I'd Drop You a Line

Materials & Tools

Card stock: assorted colors; black/white polka-dot; red

Corner rounder

Cover stock: black; yellow

Patterns: Accordion Card (pg. 104); Clothespin (pg. 103); Tiny Push Pin (pg. 103)

Pens: black felt-tipped; silver metallic

White twine

Instructions

Refer to General Instructions on pages 5–13.

1. Enlarge Accordion Card Pattern 55%. Transfer pattern onto black cover stock.

2. Transfer Tiny Push Pin Pattern onto red card stock.

3. Transfer Clothespin Pattern onto assorted colored card stocks. Repeat eight times.

4. Cut out card and designs.

5. Crease card on perforation lines, creating pleats.

6. Cut 4¼" x 5" covers from yellow card stock for front and back.

7. Using corner rounder, round corners of covers.

8. Cut two 3½" x 4¼" mats from white card stock.

9. Cut 3½" x 2¾" rectangle from polka-dot card stock. Cut mat ⅛" larger than rectangle all around from red card stock.

10. Adhere one end of card ⅛" down from top edge onto white mat. Repeat for remaining end of card and mat.

11. Center and adhere white mat onto front and back cover.

12. Adhere red mat slightly off-center onto front of cover. Center and adhere polka-dot mat onto red mat.

13. Using silver pen, color hinges of clothespins and points of push pins. Adhere one clothespin onto front of cover.

14. Cut 12" piece of twine. Adhere eight clothespins onto pleats, weaving twine among clothespins.

15. Adhere one push pin 1" from each twine end, adhering both twine and push pin onto card.

16. Cut strip from white card stock to fit horizontally inside of card. Note: The size of strip will be determined by length of message.

17. Using black pen, write desired message on strip.

18. Adhere strip onto inside of cover.

Father's Day

When closed, the accordion card appears quite ordinary; but opened, it reveals a forest of colorful designs. Above and below are two other examples for Accordion Cards.

Congratulations

Simply Tree Mendous

Materials & Tools

Barnwood patterned paper

Card stock: green; white

Cover stock: burgundy; green, 8½" x 11"

Double-sided tape

Gold metallic pen

Patterns: Accordion Card (pg. 104); Country Christmas Tree (pg. 104)

Photograph: 3⅝" x 2⅞"

Press-on letters for Tree Mendous: ¼"

Stickers: Christmas floral; tiny star (2)

Instructions

Refer to General Instructions on pages 5–13.

1. Enlarge Accordion Card Pattern 55%. Transfer pattern onto green cover stock.

2. Transfer Country Christmas Tree Pattern onto white card stock. Repeat four times.

3. Cut out card and designs.

4. Crease card on perforation lines, creating pleats.

5. Cut cover ½" larger than front and back panel of card all around from burgundy cover stock.

6. Tape one end of card ½" down from inside top of front cover. Repeat for remaining end of card and back cover. See photograph on page 14.

7. Cut tree trunks from barnwood paper. Adhere trunks onto trees. Adhere trees into three pleats as desired.

8. Place letters on inside of card for Tree Mendous message. See photograph at right.

9. Cut mat ⅛" larger than photograph all around from white card stock.

10. Center and adhere photograph onto mat. Center and adhere mat onto inside bottom of card.

11. Cut 4¼" x 3" rectangle from green card stock to decorate front cover.

12. Cut mat ⅛" larger than rectangle all around from white card stock.

13. Using gold pen, write desired message on rectangle.

14. Center and adhere rectangle onto mat. Place tiny star stickers on mat. Adhere mat onto front of cover. Place Christmas sticker on top edge of mat.

Happy Birthday

Decorated with candles and a party noisemaker, this makes the perfect birthday card for any age. Match the numbers of candles to the years old for an especially personal touch.

Pocket Cards

Pocket Cards are perfect for giving items such as money, gift certificates, or theater tickets. These cards have a pocket that sits on the cover. The pocket is adhered to the cover on the sides and bottom, but the top is left open, allowing for the inclusion of any number of special items. Be certain to create your card and envelope large enough to accommodate the size of the item that will be placed in the pocket.

If a pocket is being made for a photograph, start with a pocket large enough to hold the photograph and create the card to fit. Make certain there is an envelope sized to fit as well.

A note can always be folded to fit in a pocket, but this is not the case with a photograph.

Decorated with hearts and a simple "I Love You", this Pocket Card will be a hit with your loved one.

Making Pockets

1. Cut card stock or cover stock approximately ⅓–½ the vertical size of the cover.

2. Using glue stick, apply narrow strip of glue on sides and bottom of card.

3. Adhere pocket onto bottom front of card.

Happy Birthday

Materials & Tools

Card stock: assorted colors;
   assorted patterns; black/white
   polka-dot; gold; red; white

Cover stock: black

Pattern: Candles (pg. 106)

Pen: gold metallic

Instructions

Refer to General Instructions on pages 5–13.

1. Transfer Candles Pattern onto assorted colored and gold card stocks. Cut out candles.

2. Trim flame off of assorted colored candles and adhere onto gold candles.

3. Cut 6¼" x 9¼" card from black cover stock. Fold in half widthwise.

4. See Making Pockets on page 26. Create pocket from polka-dot card stock.

5. Cut mat ⅛" larger than pocket all around from red card stock. Center and adhere pocket onto mat.

6. Adhere 4–5 candles onto pocket, extending candle flame over top of pocket.

7. Adhere bottom and side edges of pocket onto bottom front of card, leaving room for desired item to slide inside.

8. Using gold pen, dot around candle flames.

9. Use remaining candles to decorate inside of card. Using gold pen, write birthday message.

Cute as a Button

Materials & Tools

Card stock: assorted colors; black; white; yellow

Cover stock: white

Pattern: Tiny Button (pg. 107)

Pens: black felt-tipped; silver metallic

Photograph: 3" x 5"

Ruler

Instructions

Refer to General Instructions on pages 5–13.

1. Transfer Tiny Button Pattern onto assorted colored card stocks. Repeat six times.

2. Cut out designs.

3. Cut 6¼" x 9¼" card from white cover stock. Fold in half widthwise.

4. See Making Pockets on page 26. Create pocket from black card stock.

5. Crop photograph as desired. Adhere photograph onto yellow card stock. Trim yellow card stock all around photograph as desired, creating mat. Note: Photograph will be item that is placed into pocket.

6. Adhere buttons onto top pocket edge, overlapping each other.

7. Using silver pen, draw stitch marks around pocket and thread through buttons.

8. Cut 2" x 1" strip from white card stock to fit horizontally on pocket.

9. Using black pen, write desired message on strip. Adhere strip onto bottom front of pocket.

10. Adhere bottom and side edges of pocket onto bottom front of card, leaving room for photograph to slide inside.

11. Use remaining buttons to decorate inside of card. Using black pen, write birth information.

Decorated with bandages, pills, and a stethoscope, this Pocket Card is perfect for someone feeling under the weather. Aspirin, cough drops, or candy placed in the pocket is sure to lift their spirits.

Decorated with a baseball, shirt pocket, and stars, this Pocket Card is for the sports fan in your life. The recipient will especially love the tickets to a favorite sporting event.

Happy Holidays

Materials & Tools

Card stock: gold metallic

Christmas floral sticker

Cover stock: burgundy; cream; green

Gold metallic pen

Pattern: Small Primitive Star (pg. 107)

Ruler

Instructions

Refer to General Instructions on pages 5–13.

1. Transfer Small Primitive Star Pattern onto card stock. Repeat two times.

2. Cut out designs.

3. Cut 6¼" x 9¼" card from green cover stock. Fold in half widthwise.

4. See Making Pockets on page 26. Create pocket from burgundy cover stock.

5. Cut mat ⅛" larger than pocket all around from burgundy cover stock.

6. Cut strip from burgundy cover stock to fit horizontally on pocket. Note: The size of strip will be determined by length of message.

7. Using gold pen and ruler, create border around strip. Write desired message on strip.

8. Adhere strip onto pocket. Place floral sticker on top edge of pocket.

9. Adhere bottom and side edges of pocket onto bottom front of card, leaving room for desired item to slide inside.

10. Adhere stars onto front of card.

11. Using gold pen, dot around stars.

12. Line inside of card with contrasting paper. Using gold pen, write desired message.

Pop-Up Cards

Pop-up Cards involve the cutting and folding of pop-up tabs, which allow the decorative elements inside the card to pop right off the page.

The number, size, and placement of the tabs can vary, depending on the items that will be presented on each tab. A cover is needed to conceal the notches cut in the card that make the pop-up tabs.

The pop-up format can be used for any theme, simply by substituting other designs for the hearts. It is equally effective to decorate each pop-up tab with stickers, photographs, craft punch art, or rubber-stamped designs. In any case, the insides are hidden until the recipient opens the card. The pop-up tabs then spring to life, catching the unsuspecting recipient by surprise.

I Love You

Materials & Tools

Adhesive foam dots

Black felt-tipped pen

Card stock: assorted patterns; black; black/white pin-dot; white

Cover stock: red; white

Patterns: Arrow (pg. 106); Lollipop Alphabet (pg. 125); Pop-Up #1 (pg. 106); Pop-Up #3 (pg. 106); Primitive Hearts (pg. 107)

Ruler

Stickers: checkered strips; hearts; polka-dot strips

Instructions

Refer to General Instructions on pages 5–13.

1. Enlarge Pop-Up #1 Pattern 50%. Enlarge Pop-Up #3 Pattern 50%.

2. Transfer Arrow Pattern onto pin-dot card stock.

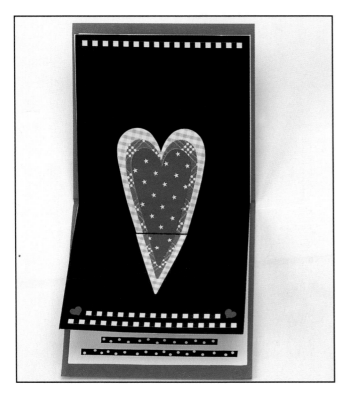

3. Transfer Pop-Up #1 Pattern onto white cover stock, creating card #1. Repeat with black card stock, creating card #2.

4. Transfer Pop-Up #3 Pattern onto white card stock, creating card #3.

5. Transfer Lollipop Alphabet Pattern for i, YOU, and Primitive Hearts Pattern onto patterned card stocks. Repeat for Primitive Hearts. Note: Enlarge letters for i and YOU as desired.

6. Cut out cards, designs, and letters.

7. Crease cards and pop-up tabs on perforation lines.

8. Adhere i onto black card stock. Trim, leaving $\frac{1}{16}$" border.

9. Adhere i onto pop-up tab of card #1.

10. Cut dot for i from assorted card stock. Repeat four times, getting successively smaller. Layer and adhere dots together, largest to smallest.

11. Place layered dot on foam dot. Adhere onto inside of card above i. Place polka-dot strip stickers $\frac{1}{8}$" from top and bottom on card #1.

12. Layer and adhere three heart designs together, largest to smallest. Repeat for remaining three hearts.

13. Adhere back of one heart set onto pop-up tab of card #2. Crease bottom of heart to match crease at bottom of pop-up card. Cut heart off at crease and adhere below crease of pop-up. See photograph at top left.

14. Place checkered strip stickers $\frac{1}{8}$" from top and bottom of card #2.

15. Cut YOU from assorted card stock. Adhere each letter onto black card stock. Cut around each letter, leaving $\frac{1}{16}$" border. Note: Leave center of O solid.

16. Adhere heart stickers to O. Adhere bottom back of letters onto pop-up tabs of card #3.
Continued on page 34.

Continued from page 33.

17. Place polka-dot strip stickers ⅛" in from top and bottom of card #3.

18. Adhere bottom of first card to top of second card. Adhere bottom of second card to top of third card. Note: This process can be repeated, adding as many pages as desired.

19. Cut 4½" x 8½ cover from red cover stock.

20. Fold cover, creating spine to accommodate thickness of inside pages.

21. Adhere card cover to pop up book, leaving narrow border all around.

22. Cut 4¼" x 4" rectangle from black card stock for front of cover.

23. Adhere remaining layered hearts onto rectangle as desired.

24. Adhere arrow onto red card stock. Trim, leaving 1⁄16" border. Cut arrow in half.

25. Using black pen and ruler, draw lines on center of heart to look like slits.

26. Place one foam dot behind tip of arrow and base of arrow. Match and place front half of arrow onto right slit line. Match and place back half of arrow onto left slit line, leaving open space in middle.

27. Center and adhere black rectangle onto front of cover.

28. Place heart stickers inside of card as desired.

You're Invited

Materials & Tools

Adhesive foam dots

Black felt-tipped pen

Black ink pad

Card stock: assorted colors; green/ white pin-dot; red; white; yellow

Cover stock: black; white

Patterns: Balloons (pg. 109); Noise-maker (pg. 109); Pop-Up #1 (pg. 106); Splash (pg. 109)

Rubber stamp: invitation

Ruler

Instructions

Refer to General Instructions on pages 5–13.

1. Enlarge Pop-Up #1 Pattern 50%. Transfer pattern onto white cover stock.

2. Transfer Balloons Pattern and Noisemaker Pattern onto assorted colored card stock.

3. Transfer Splash Pattern onto pin-dot card stock and yellow card stock.

4. Cut out card and designs. Embellish noisemaker as desired.

5. Adhere pin-dot splash onto noise-maker. Center and place foam dot on back of yellow splash. Place yellow splash on top of pin-dot splash.

6. Crease card and pop-up tab on perforation lines.

7. Adhere round balloon onto pop-up tab as desired. Adhere one heart balloon onto top edge of round balloon.

8. Adhere assorted colored balloons onto back of card.

9. Using black pen, draw balloon strings.

10. Cut 2¾" x 1½" rectangle from white card stock.

11. Cut mat ⅛" larger than rectangle all around from red card stock.

12. Using ink pad and rubber stamp, stamp image onto white rectangle. Center and adhere white rectangle onto red mat.

13. Adhere mat onto bottom inside of card.

14. Cut cover ⅛" larger than card all around from black cover stock. Fold in half widthwise.

15. Cut 4¼" x 3¾" rectangle from white card stock.

16. Adhere noisemaker onto white rectangle.

17. Using black pen and ruler, create border around rectangle. Write desired message on rectangle.

18. Adhere rectangle onto front of cover. Center and adhere cover onto card.

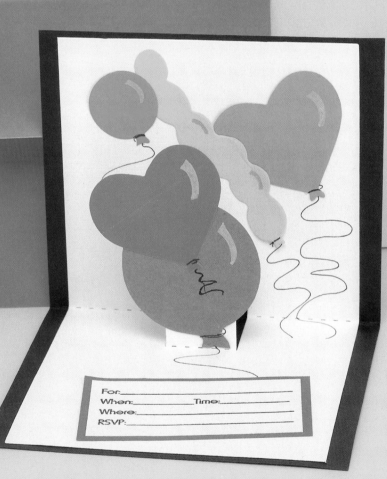

What's Up?

Materials & Tools

Card stock: blue; green; orange; red

Cover stock: white; yellow

Black felt-tipped pen

Border stickers: ⅟₁₆"

Orange marker

Patterns: Carrot (pg. 107); Multiple Pop-Up #2 (pg. 108)

Press-on letters for What's Up?

Ruler

Instructions

Refer to General Instructions on pages 5–13.

1. Enlarge Multiple Pop-Up #2 Pattern 44%. Transfer pattern onto white cover stock.

2. Transfer Carrot Pattern onto orange card stock. Repeat seven times.

3. Transfer top only of Carrot Pattern onto green card stock. Repeat seven times.

4. Cut out card and designs.

5. Crease card and pop-up tabs on perforation lines.

6. Using orange marker, shade carrots as desired.

7. Adhere green tops onto carrots.

8. Adhere carrots onto pop-up tabs.

9. Cut 4⅛" x 1⅛" rectangle from green card stock.

10. Using black pen and ruler, create border around rectangle. Write desired message on rectangle.

11. Adhere rectangle onto bottom inside of card. Place border stickers around top and bottom edges of card.

12. Cut 7½" x 10½" cover from yellow cover stock. Fold in half widthwise.

13. Adhere card onto inside of cover, matching folds.

14. Cut 4⅜" x 2½" rectangle from blue card stock.

15. Cut mat ⅛₆" larger than rectangle all around from red card stock.

16. Place letters on rectangle for What's Up?

17. Center and adhere rectangle onto mat. Center and adhere mat onto front of cover. Adhere remaining carrot onto front of mat as desired.

Invitation

Materials & Tools

Adhesive foam dots

Black felt-tipped pen

Black ink pad

Card stock: black/white checkered; green; orange; white; yellow

Cover stock: black

Craft punch: moon

Patterns: Ghost #2 (pg. 106); Multiple Pop-Up #1 (pg. 108); Tiny Pumpkin (pg. 106)

Rubber stamp: invitation

Ruler

Stickers: pumpkin; gerber daisy

Instructions

Refer to General Instructions on pages 5–13.

1. Enlarge Multiple Pop-Up Pattern 39%. Transfer pattern onto black cover stock.

2. Transfer Ghost #2 Pattern onto white card stock.

3. Transfer Tiny Pumpkin Pattern onto orange card stock. Repeat three times. Repeat four times with green card stock.

4. Cut out card and designs. Embellish pumpkins.

5. Crease card and pop-up tabs on perforation lines.

6. Adhere pumpkins onto pop-up tabs as desired. Place pumpkin sticker on remaining pop-up tab.

7. Cut 6" x 9" cover from from checkered card stock.

8. Cut cover ⅛" larger than checkered cover all around from black cover stock. Center and adhere checkered cover onto black cover, creating two-sided cover. Fold in half widthwise. Center and adhere card to cover.

9. Cut 2⅞" x 1½" rectangle from white card stock. Cut mat ¹⁄₁₆ larger than rectangle all around from orange card stock.

10. Using black ink pad and rubber stamp, stamp image onto rectangle.

Fill in information as desired. Center and adhere onto mat.

11. Adhere mat onto bottom left inside of card.

12. Cut 3¾" x 1" rectangle from yellow card stock.

13. Cut mat ¼" larger than rectangle all around from orange card stock.

14. Using black pen and ruler, create border around rectangle and around mat. Write desired message on rectangle.

15. Center and adhere rectangle onto mat. Adhere mat onto left top corner of card cover.

16. Cut two ¹⁄₁₆" x 6" and two ¹⁄₁₆" x 4½" strips from orange card stock Adhere strips around all four sides on front of cover.

17. Using craft punch, punch out four moons. Adhere one moon onto each front corner of cover.

18. Adhere one ghost onto front of cover. Place foam dots behind remaining ghost. Place ghost onto front of cover, overlapping first ghost.

19. Place daisy sticker in ghost's hand.

For:_____
When:_____
Where:_____ Time:_____
RSVP:_____

Photo Cards

Adding a photograph to a card instantly personalizes the greeting. Even the simplest of cards becomes more special with the inclusion of a photograph.

These Photo Cards are created with paper or cover stock that is two-sided—the two colors or patterns being compatible, but not identical.

The photograph at right shows the front and back of the card made from two-sided card stock before creasing on perforation lines.

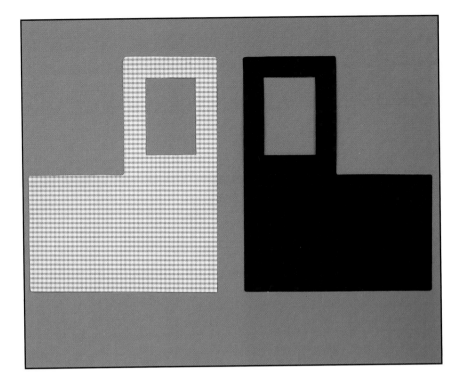

It is easy to create two-sided paper, using spray adhesive, adhesive sheets, or a Xyron machine that applies adhesive to full sheets of paper. Two-sided card stock is also available as well as two-sided gift wrap.

Once the paper is two-sided, the Picture Frame Fold Up is cut and creased on the perforation lines. The addition of themed designs or stickers and fancy pens is all that is needed for a super simple Photo Card. See photograph at left.

These Photo Cards fold flat for mailing, but sit up perfectly when removed from the envelope.

Springtime

Materials & Tools

Card stock: assorted coordinating patterns; cream/green patterned, two-sided

Double-sided tape

Pattern: Picture Frame Fold Up Card (pg. 110)

Photograph

Stickers: bow; floral

Instructions

Refer to General Instructions on pages 5–13.

1. Enlarge Picture Frame Fold Up Card Pattern 74%. Transfer pattern onto two-sided card stock.

2. Cut out card. Using craft knife, cut out frame opening.

3. Fold card on perforation lines.

4. Crop photograph to fit into frame as desired. Tape photograph to back of frame visible through frame. Tape sides and bottom of frame to back of card.

5. Cut 3" x 2" rectangle and 3" x 1" rectangle from assorted card stocks. Butt edges of rectangles together adhere onto inside front of cover. See photograph above.

6. Place floral sticker on top of mat. Place bow sticker on inside edges of rectangles.

40

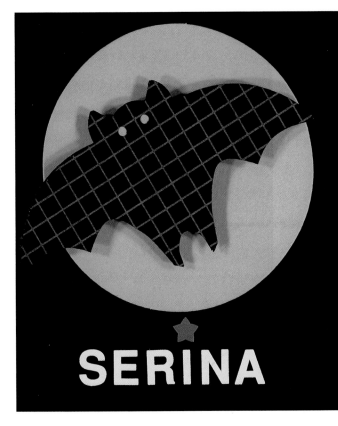

Halloween

Materials & Tools

Adhesive foam dots

Card stock: black patterned; black/orange/ white patterned, two-sided; yellow

Double-sided tape

Hole punch: 1/8"

Patterns: Bat (pg. 110); Picture Frame Fold Up Card (pg. 110)

Photograph

Press-on letters for desired message: 3/8"

Tiny star stickers (optional)

Instructions

Refer to General Instructions on pages 5–13.

1. Enlarge Picture Frame Fold Up Card Pattern 74%. Transfer pattern onto two-sided card stock.

2. Transfer Bat Pattern onto black patterned card stock.

3. Cut out card and designs. Using craft knife, cut out frame opening.

4. Crease card on perforation lines.

5. Cut 3"-diameter circle from yellow card stock.

Continued on page 42.

Continued from page 41.

6. Adhere a piece of yellow card stock onto inside of back cover behind frame opening.

7. Crop photograph to fit inside frame as desired. Tape photograph to inside back of card so it appears to sit on edge of frame. Tape sides and bottom of frame to inside back of card.

8. Adhere circle onto inside front of cover for moon.

9. Using hole punch, punch two circles from yellow card stock. Adhere circles onto bat for eyes.

10. Place foam dots on back of bat. Place bat on moon.

11. Center and place letters below moon for desired message. Tip: If desired message contains an "i"(s), dot with tiny star sticker(s).

Happy Hanukkah

Materials & Tools

Adhesive foam dots

Card stock: dk. brown; lt. brown; gold metallic; gold metallic/white patterned, two-sided; purple

Double-sided tape

Gold metallic pen

Patterns: Dreidel (pg. 110); Picture Frame Fold Up Card (pg. 110)

Instructions

Refer to General Instructions on pages 5–13.

1. Enlarge Picture Frame Fold Up Card Pattern 74%. Transfer pattern onto two-sided card stock.

2. Transfer Dreidel Pattern onto metallic card stock.

3. Cut out card and designs. Using craft knife, cut out frame opening. Embellish dreidel as desired with dk. brown and lt. brown card stock.

4. Crease frame on perforation lines.

5. Adhere embellishments onto dreidel as desired.

6. Crop photograph to fit into frame as desired. Tape photograph to back of frame, visible through frame. Tape sides and bottom of frame to back of card.

7. Cut 2¾" x ¾" rectangle from purple card stock.

8. Using gold pen, write desired message on rectangle.

9. Cut mat ⅛" larger than rectangle all around from metallic card stock. Center and adhere rectangle onto mat. Center and adhere mat ¼" down from front top edge of card.

10. Place foam dots on back of dreidel. Place dreidel at left front of cover. Center and adhere message above dreidel.

These Photo Cards are created so that they will stand up when folded. What a quick and easy way to decorate a desk or bedside table.

Window Cards

The cover of a Window Card has an opening that allows some of the decorative elements inside of the card to show through. The size and shape of the window can vary.

A craft knife is the most effect way to cut out the window. Note: A ruler helps in keeping a straight edge. See photograph at right.

It is also effective to double or triple the number of folds so that multiple window openings can overlap each other on the front of the card. See Multiple Window Cards below.

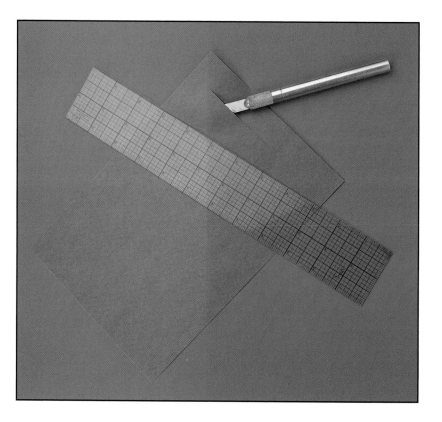

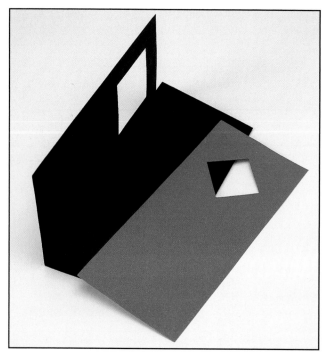

Multiple Window Cards

The Geometric Tri-Fold is folded into thirds so that one window opening remains on the front of cover, the second window opening shows through the first, and the base is solid. The folds of a Multiple Window Card can be lined with a different color. See photograph at left.

Too Cool

Materials & Tools

Adhesive foam dots

Card stock: black; craft; red

Craft knife

Pattern: Tiny Heart (pg. 109);

Pens: black felt-tipped; gold metallic

Ruler

Tiny gold star stickers (3)

Instructions

Refer to General Instructions on pages 5–13.

1. Transfer Tiny Heart Pattern onto red card stock. Repeat five times.

2. Cut out designs.

3. Cut 9⅛" x 6¼" rectangle from black card stock. Repeat with craft card stock.

4. Adhere black card stock onto craft card stock for two-sided card stock. Black is outside. Fold in half widthwise.

5. Using craft knife cut 2¾" square in card. See photograph.

6. Using black pen and ruler, create border through window on inside of card, slightly smaller than window.

7. Using gold pen, write desired messages on hearts.

8. Place foam dots on back of some of hearts. Place hearts inside border, overlapping hearts as desired.

9. Place gold star stickers on front of cover. See photograph.

Birthday Card

Materials & Tools

Adhesive foam dots

Card stock: assorted colors

Cover stock: black

Craft knife

Craft punch: balloon, small

Pattern: Balloons (pg. 113)

Ruler

Silver metallic pen

Instructions

Refer to General Instructions on pages 5–13.

1. Transfer Balloons Pattern as desired onto assorted colored card stock.

2. Cut out designs.

3. Cut 9⅛" x 6¼" rectangle from black cover stock. Fold in half widthwise.

4. Using craft knife, cut out 2¾" square in card. See photograph.

5. Draw highlights for balloons onto assorted colored card stock. Cut out highlights. Adhere highlights onto balloons.

6. Adhere oval balloon onto large balloon.

7. Place foam dots on back of large balloon. Place balloon on inside of card, visible through window.

8. Adhere remaining balloon onto inside of card.

9. Using silver pen, draw balloon strings. Close card.

10. Using silver pen and ruler, create border around window. Write desired message on front of card.

11. Using craft punch, punch balloons from assorted colored card stock. Adhere balloons onto front of card.

12. Using silver pen, draw balloon strings.

Swim Party

Materials & Tools

Card stock: assorted colors; white; yellow

Cover stock: blue

Craft knife

Patterns: Fin (pg.112); Snorkel and Mask (pg. 112)

Pens: blue felt-tipped; silver metallic

Plastic page protector

Instructions

Refer to General Instructions on pages 5–13.

1. Transfer Fin Pattern onto assorted colored card stock.

2. Transfer Snorkel and Mask Pattern onto assorted colored card stock. Repeat two times.

3. Cut out designs.

4. Cut 9⅛" x 6¼" rectangle from blue cover stock. Fold in half widthwise.

5. Using craft knife, cut out 2¾" square in card. See photograph.

6. Sandwich strip of plastic cut from plastic page protector between card stock masks. Match and adhere together. Adhere completed mask onto snorkel.

7. Cut 4¼" x 6" rectangle from yellow card stock. Adhere rectangle onto inside of card.

8. Cut 3½" x 2" rectangle from white card stock. Using blue pen, write party information on rectangle. Adhere rectangle onto inside bottom of card.

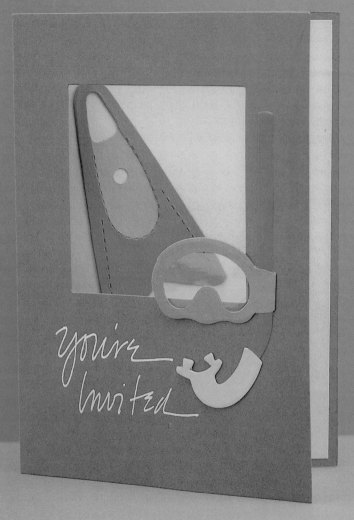

9. Adhere fin onto inside of card, visible through window.

10. Using silver pen, write desired message on front of card.

11. Adhere snorkel and mask onto front of card, overlapping window.

Merry Christmoose

Materials & Tools

Card stock: red; white

Craft knife

Felt-tipped pens: assorted colors

Patterns: Accordion Fold #1
  (pg. 103); Moose (pg. 112)

Transparent tape

Instructions

Refer to General Instructions on
pages 5–13.

1. Enlarge Accordion Fold #1
Pattern 34%. Transfer pattern
onto red card stock.

2. Transfer Moose Pattern onto
white card stock. Repeat two
times.

3. Cut out Accordion Fold and
designs.

4. Cut two 5½" x 8" covers from
red card stock for front and back.

5. Using craft knife, cut 4" square in one cover.

6. Crease folds on perforation lines, creating pleats. Cut accordion fold into two sections to make sides of card. Note: Each section should have three pleats with a tab on each end.

7. Tape one end of fold on inside edge of front cover. Repeat for remaining fold at opposite edge of front cover. See photograph at right.

8. Adhere one moose onto inside front cover, visible through window.

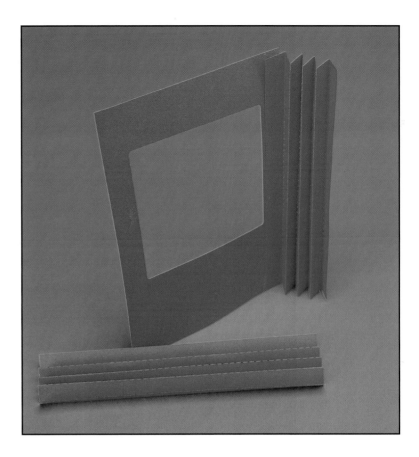

9. Adhere second moose onto 5¼" x 3" rectangle. Tape rectangle into first pleat, facing moose in opposite direction of first moose. See photograph at left.

10. Adhere third moose onto 5¼" x 3" rectangle. Tape rectangle into second pleat, facing second moose in opposite direction.

11. Tape one end of fold on inside edge of back cover. Repeat for remaining fold at opposite edge of back cover. See photograph at left.

12. Cut 4" x 2" rectangle from white card stock.

13. Using assorted felt-tipped pens, write desired message on rectangle. Decorate as desired. Adhere rectangle below window onto front of card.

Rose
Window

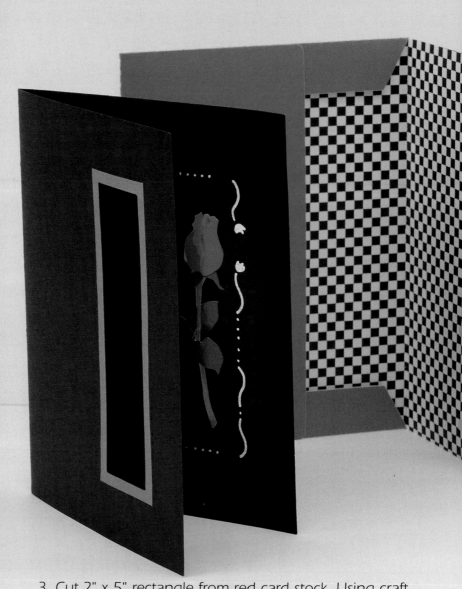

Materials & Tools

Card stock: red

Cover stock: black

Craft knife

Rose sticker

Ruler

Silver metallic pen

Instructions

Refer to General
Instructions on pages 5–13.

1. Cut 6¼" x 9¼" rectangle
from black cover stock. Fold
in half widthwise.

2. Using craft knife, cut out
1½" x 4½" window. See
photograph.

3. Cut 2" x 5" rectangle from red card stock. Using craft
knife, cut out inside of rectangle, leaving red frame.

4. Adhere red frame onto window. See photograph.

5. Center and adhere rose sticker visible through
window.

6. Using silver pen and ruler, create border around rose.

Feeling Down?

Materials & Tools

Black felt-tipped pen

Card stock: black; green; magenta; orange; yellow

Cover stock: blue

Craft knife

Craft punches: stem border; sun

Hole punch: ¼"

Pattern: Window Card #8 (pg. 111)

Ruler

Instructions

Refer to General Instructions on pages 5–13.

1. Cut 6¼" x 9¼" rectangle from blue cover stock. Fold in half widthwise.

2. Transfer Window Card #8 Pattern onto blue cover stock. See photograph.

3. Using craft knife, cut out window.

4. Use window shape to create a narrow border from magenta card stock. Cut out shape.

5. Adhere border onto window.

6. Using craft punch, punch out seven suns from yellow card stock. Repeat seven times on orange card stock.

7. Using hole punch, punch seven circles from black card stock.

8. Overlap and adhere one yellow sun onto one orange sun, creating sunflowers. Note: Sunflowers can be cut in half for a different look.

9. Center and adhere black circles onto sunflowers.

10. Using craft punch, punch out seven stems from green card stock.

11. Cut 2½" x 6¼" rectangle from yellow card stock.

12. Using black pen and ruler, create border around rectangle. Write desired message on rectangle.

13. Adhere rectangle ½" up from bottom front edge of card.

Baby Announcement

Materials & Tools

Burgundy ink pad

Card stock: assorted patterns; burgundy

Cover stock: cream

Craft knife

Craft punch: feet

Gold metallic pen

Patterns: Baby Rattle (pg. 112); Geometric Tri-Fold #2 (pg. 111)

Rubber stamp: baby announcement

Ruler

Instructions

Refer to General Instructions on pages 5–13.

1. Enlarge Geometric Tri-Fold #2 Pattern 56%. Transfer pattern onto cream cover stock.

2. Transfer Baby Rattle Pattern onto patterned card stock.

3. Cut out card and design. Using craft knife, cut out windows.

4. Crease card on perforation lines, folding in second layer of card first.

5. Using gold pen and ruler, create border around square window on front of card.

6. Line second layer of card with the diamond opening with complementary patterned card stock.

7. Line each section of inside of card with burgundy card stock, leaving cream border around each section.

8. Cut 3¼" x 4¾" rectangle from cream cover stock.

9. Using gold pen and ruler, create border around rectangle.

10. Using rubber stamp and burgundy ink pad, stamp image on rectangle. Fill in information as desired.

11. Using burgundy ink pad and your thumb, stamp image of your thumb on cream cover stock. Repeat. Using craft punch, punch out two feet from stamped thumb prints.

12. Center and adhere feet onto inside center section of card, visible through window.

13. Using gold pen, trace around feet as desired.

14. Adhere baby rattle onto front of card below square window.

Our New Baby

Name..
Date..
Time..
Weight..
Length..
Parents..

Dad

Materials & Tools

Black felt-tipped pen

Card stock: black; black/white pin-dot; blue; green; red; white; yellow

Cover stock: craft

Craft knife

Patterns: Fishing Pole (pg. 113); Geometric Tri-Fold #2 (pg. 111); Lollipop Alphabet for DAD (pg. 125); Tiny Fish (pg. 113)

Ruler

Instructions

Refer to General Instructions on pages 5–13.

1. Enlarge Geometric Tri-Fold #2 Pattern 56%. Transfer pattern onto craft card stock.

2. Transfer Fishing Pole onto black card stock.

3. Transfer Lollipop Alphabet Pattern for DAD onto pin-dot card stock. Note: Enlarge letters as desired.

4. Transfer Tiny Fish Pattern onto green card stock. Repeat with yellow card stock.

5. Cut out card and designs. Embellish fishing pole as desired. Using craft knife, cut out windows.

6. Crease card on perforation lines, folding in second layer of card first.

7. Using black pen and ruler, create border around square window on front of card.

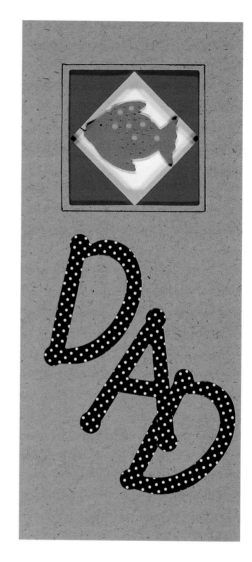

8. Line second layer of card with diamond opening with red card stock.

9. Line inside center of card with white card stock.

10. Using craft knife, poke holes in green fish, varying sizes. Using black pen, draw one eye on green fish.

11. Adhere green fish onto top of yellow fish. Center and adhere fish onto inside center of card, visible through window.

12. Adhere fishing pole onto inside center of card. Using black pen, draw fishing line from pole to fish's mouth as desired.

13. Cut 2" x ¾" rectangle from red card stock.

14. Using black pen and ruler, create border around rectangle. Write desired message on rectangle.

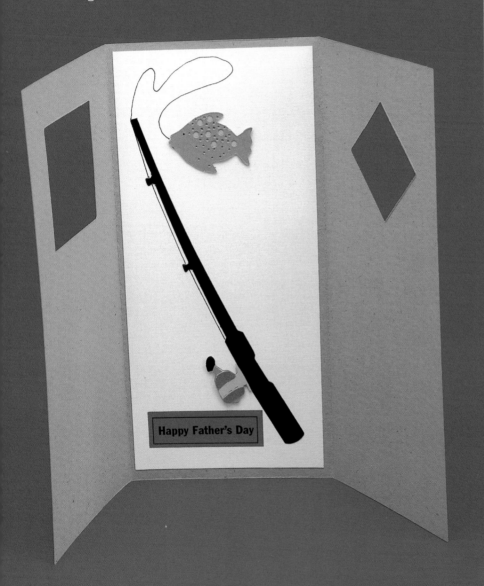

Happy Father's Day

15. Adhere rectangle onto bottom inside center of card.

16. Adhere "Dad" below square window onto front of card.

Thank You

Materials & Tools

Black felt-tipped pen

Card stock: assorted patterns; craft; cream; leaf patterned (solid on reverse side)

Craft knife

Patterns: Geometric Tri-Fold #2 (pg.111); Tiny Heart (pg.109)

Ruler

Instructions

Refer to General Instructions on pages 5–13.

1. Enlarge Geometric Tri-Fold #2 Pattern 56%. Transfer pattern onto leaf patterned card stock.

2. Transfer Tiny Heart Pattern onto red patterned card stock.
Continued on page 56.

Continued from page 55.

3. Cut out card and design. Using craft knife, cut out windows from card.

4. Crease card on perforation lines, folding in second layer of card first.

5. Line second layer of card with diamond opening with craft card stock.

6. Cut 1¾" x ¾" rectangle from leaf patterned card stock.

7. Cut mat ⅟₁₆" larger than rectangle from cream card stock.

8. Cut second mat ⅟₁₆" larger than first mat from craft card stock.

9. Center and adhere smaller mat onto larger mat.

10. Using black pen, write desired message onto rectangle. Center and adhere rectangle onto mat.

11. Using black pen and ruler, create border around rectangle on mat.

12. Center and adhere heart onto inside center fold of card, visible through window.

13. Using black pen and ruler, create diamond-shaped border around heart.

Vellum Cards

Vellum is a specialty paper product that helps to create a particularly unique effect in card making. It is available in a variety of weights, colors, and textures with some being more "see-through" than others. See photograph at right.

It is easy to run vellum through a computer printer or color copy machine, making it possible to copy a photograph or print an entire wedding event onto vellum. See photographs below.

In each case, the vellum's filmy quality allows the item that is placed beneath to show through in a very special way.

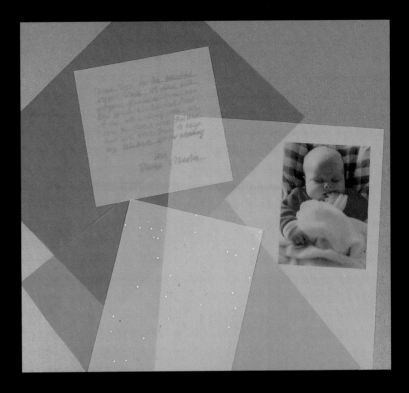

★MARLIE★

Running vellum through a color copier or computer printer will result in considerable savings as compared to a commercial printer. It is possible to print the text on vellum which sits over the photograph or color copy the photograph onto vellum which sits over the text.

Materials & Tools

Black felt-tipped pen

Card stock: beige patterned; lt. brown; dk. camel; lt. camel; white

Craft knife

Floral sticker

Pattern: Window Card #5 (pg. 114)

Ruler

Talcum powder

Vellum

We've Moved

Instructions

Refer to General Instructions on pages 5–13.

1. Enlarge Window Card #5 Pattern 65%. Transfer pattern onto beige patterned card stock. Cut out card. Using craft knife, cut out windows.

2. Transfer area between perforated lines for windowpanes onto white card stock. Cut out design. Using craft knife, cut out windows.

3. Crease card on perforation lines.

4. Sandwich vellum between white windowpanes and windowpanes on card. Match and adhere.

5. Cut 3¼" x 1" rectangle from lt. brown card stock.

6. Using black pen and ruler, create border around rectangle.

7. Adhere rectangle under window. Open center window. Place floral sticker on top edge of rectangle, extending over window.

8. Using fingers, brush powder on back side of sticker where it extends over window box.

9. Cut 4⅜" x 6" rectangle from lt. camel card stock. Center and adhere rectangle onto inside back of card.

10. Cut 3" x ½" rectangle from lt. camel card stock.

11. Using black pen, write desired message on rectangle.

12. Cut mat ⅛" larger than rectangle all around from dk. camel card stock.

13. Center and adhere rectangle onto mat. Center and adhere mat onto top inside of back card.

Love

Materials & Tools

Black embroidery floss

Card stock: black;
   cream; gold metallic

Cover stock: black

Craft knife

Hole punch: ⅛"

Gold metallic pen

Pattern: Tiny Heart (pg. 109)

Ruler

Vellum or handmade transparent paper

Instructions

Refer to General Instructions on pages 5–13.

1. Cut 3" x 1½" rectangle from metallic card stock. Transfer Tiny Heart Pattern onto metallic rectangle. Repeat. Using craft knife, carefully cut out design, saving rectangle.

2. Cut 6⅜" x 9⅜" cover from black cover stock. Fold in half widthwise.

3. Center and adhere rectangle onto cover. Using gold pen and ruler, create border around rectangle.

4. Cut 6" x 9" cover from vellum or handmade paper. Fold cover in half widthwise. Place vellum cover over black cover, matching folds.

5. Using hole punch, pierce one hole 1¾" in from end of fold. Repeat for remaining end of fold through both vellum and card.

6. Cut 6" x 4½" rectangle from cream card stock for inside of card.

7. Center and adhere rectangle onto inside back of cover.

8. Cut 20" piece of embroidery floss. Thread each end of floss through holes to inside of card. Tie into bow.

Materials & Tools

Card stock: dk. camel; lt. camel; cream

Color copy of photograph: 5" x 4" (Option #2)

Color copy of photograph on vellum: 5" x 4" (Option #1)

Craft knife

Double-sided tape

Floral stickers (2)

Patterns: Overlapping Card A (pg. 115); Overlapping Card B (pg. 115)

Engagement Announcement

Instructions

Refer to General Instructions on pages 5–13.

1. Enlarge Overlapping Card A Pattern 51%. Enlarge Overlapping Card B Pattern 51%.

2. Transfer Card A Pattern onto dk. camel card stock.

3. Transfer Card B Pattern onto lt. camel card stock.

4. Cut out cards. Using craft knife, cut slits. Fold cards in half widthwise.

5. Overlap and tape one half of each card to each other. See photograph.

Option #1

6. Print desired message to fit on 5¼" x 4¼" rectangle from cream card stock. Cut 5¼" x 4¼" rectangle with desired message.

7. Center and adhere top edge of vellum color copy of photograph onto top edge of rectangle. Center and adhere rectangle onto center inside of card.

8. Place bottom of floral sticker on top edge of rectangle.

9. Close card with pointed end sliding through bottom slits. Place floral sticker at end of flap to secure.

Option #2

10. Cut 5¼" x 4¼" rectangle from cream card stock.

11. Center and adhere color copy of photograph onto rectangle. Center and adhere onto inside of card.

12. Print desired message to fit 5½" x 4½" rectangle of vellum. Cut 5½" x 4½" rectangle with message.

13. Place vellum over top of color copy. Place bottom of floral sticker at top center edge of vellum, attaching vellum to card.

14. Close card with pointed end sliding through bottom slits. Place floral sticker at end of flap to secure.

Darren Frederick Gogolan
and
Marlie Bennett Stewart
announce their
Engagement

The Wedding is planned for
early June
with a Honeymoon in Hawaii
They plan to reside in
Huntington Beach, California

Two options are shown for the same card: one with the photograph color-copied onto vellum and text printed on cream-colored paper, and the other with the text printed on vellum and the photograph color-copied onto cream-colored card stock.

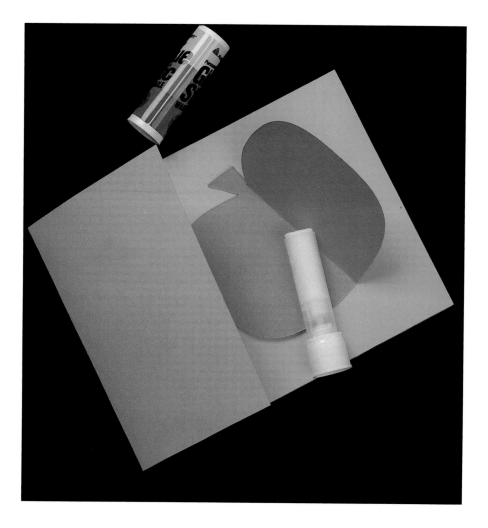

Tie It Up Cards

Tie It Up Cards are closed with a ribbon, string, or tie of some sort. Each card is folded on both sides and the card ends meet in the middle. A shape (geometric or decorative) is cut in pairs, folded identically and adhered over each end of the card. See photograph at left. This creates the look of one whole shape on the card front. It is possible to vary the look slightly by substituting a paper element that overlaps the middle seam in place of the ribbon.

This Tie It Up Card is decorated with red hearts and a single red rose sticker. It is the perfect card to tell the one that you love thanks for all they do.

Heart in a Diamond

Materials & Tools

Card stock: cream;
  dk. green; green
  flecked; green floral
  with cream back

Green felt-tipped pen

Ruler

Stickers: bow; floral;
  gold heart

Instructions

Refer to General Instruc-
tions on pages 5–13.

1. Cut 7¾" x 10 ¾" card
from green floral card
stock. Fold widthwise,
meeting two ends in
middle.

2. Cut two 3¾" squares
from dk. green card
stock.

3. Cut two squares ¹⁄₁₆"
smaller than dk. green
squares from green
flecked card stock.

4. Center and adhere
smaller squares onto
larger squares. Fold
squares in half dia-
gonally.

5. Adhere inside half of each square to inside
flaps, leaving outside half of squares loose.
Close card.

6. Cut 3¼" x ¾" rectangle from green floral card
stock.

7. Cut mat ¹⁄₁₆" larger than rectangle all around
from cream card stock.

8. Cut 3" x ¹⁄₁₆" strip from dk. green card stock.

9. Center and adhere strip onto rectangle.
Center and place heart sticker on strip.
Continued on page 64.

Continued from page 63.

10. Center and adhere rectangle onto mat. Center and adhere left half of mat onto left square, leaving rectangle loose on remaining side. See photograph on page 63.

11. Cut 3¾" x 4¼" rectangle from green flecked card stock.

12. Center and adhere rectangle ¾" down from top inside of card.

13. Using green pen and ruler, create border around rectangle. Place floral sticker over top edge of rectangle.

14. Cut 3¾" x ⅛" and 3¼" x ⅛" strips from dk. green card stock.

15. Center and adhere strips below rectangle as desired. Place bow sticker below strips.

Broken Heart

Materials & Tools

Card stock: blue; cream; cream/blue patterned; yellow; yellow/white checkered

Pattern: Bandage (pg. 115)

Stickers: floral; tiny heart

Instructions

Refer to General Instructions on pages 5–13.

1. Transfer Bandage Pattern onto yellow card stock.

2. Cut out designs.

3. Cut 4¾" x 4¼" heart from yellow/white checkered card stock. Repeat.

4. Cut 9½" x 6" card from cream/blue patterned card stock that is plain on reverse side. Fold widthwise, meeting two ends in middle.

5. Fold hearts in half. Adhere inside half of each heart to inside flaps, leaving outside half loose. Close card.

6. Place floral sticker along bottom edge of heart on outside flap.

7. Cut mat from blue card stock ⅛" larger than bandage all around.

8. Adhere bandage onto mat. Place heart sticker on bandage. Adhere half of bandage onto heart, leaving other half loose.

9. Cut 5½" x 4¼" rectangle from yellow card stock.

10. Adhere rectangle onto inside middle of card. Place floral sticker at center top of rectangle.

Hi

Materials & Tools

Black felt-tipped pen

Brads (2)

Card stock: black; craft; red

Craft paper: black/craft patterned; black/gold metallic patterned; gold metallic

Double-sided tape

Embroidery thread (12")

Hole punch: ¼"

Press-on letters for Hi: 2"

Instructions

Refer to General Instructions on pages 5–13.

1. Draw 4" circle onto black/craft patterned craft paper. Repeat.

2. Draw 1" circle onto red card stock. Repeat.

3. Cut out designs.

4. Cut 11" x 8" card from craft card stock. Fold widthwise, meeting two ends in middle.

5. Cut two mats ¼" larger than large circles all around from black card stock. Adhere circles onto mats.

6. Cut two 2" squares from metallic gold craft paper. Adhere square onto each large circle.
Continued on page 66.

Continued from page 65.

7. Fold large circles in half so gold square on top is folded diagonally. Position large folded circles over card flaps. Close card.

8. Place small red circles on top of gold triangles. See photograph.

9. Using hole punch, punch hole through small circles, outside half of large circles, and flaps. Do not punch hole through inside half of circles.

13. Cut 2½" square from black/gold patterned craft paper.

14. Cut mat from metallic craft paper ⅛" larger than square all around. Adhere square onto mat.

15. Cut 7¾" x 5¼" rectangle from black card stock. Adhere rectangle to inside middle of card. Adhere matted square onto center top of rectangle.

16. Place letters inside square for Hi.

10. Insert brad through each hole. Bend ends to close.

11. Tape inside circles to flaps, covering brad ends.

12. Using black pen, color tops of brads.

17. Tie slip knot at one end of thread. Pull thread to close knot, under small red circle. Knot other end of thread. Wrap end around opposite brad to close card.

Halloween Invitation

Materials & Tools

Black felt-tipped pen

Black satin ribbon: ¼"-wide (1 yd.)

Card stock: black; green; orange; orange/white checkered; yellow

Craft knife

Orange craft paper

Patterns: Pumpkin (pg. 113); Tiny Pumpkin (pg. 106)

Instructions

Refer to General Instructions on pages 5–13.

1. Transfer Pumpkin Pattern onto orange craft paper. Repeat.

2. Transfer Tiny Pumpkin Pattern onto orange card stock. Repeat two times.

3. Transfer pumpkin's and tiny pumpkin's stems onto green card stock. Repeat.

4. Cut out designs.

5. Cut 14" x 5½" card from yellow card stock. Fold widthwise, meeting two ends in middle.

6. Adhere green pumpkin stems onto orange pumpkin stems.

Continued on page 68.

For:_____
When:_____ Time:_____
Where:_____
RSVP:_____

Continued from page 67.

7. Using craft knife, cut ¾" slit in right side of one pumpkin and left side of other pumpkin. See photograph on page 67.

8. Fold pumpkins in half widthwise. Adhere inside of each pumpkin to inside flaps of card, leaving outside half of pumpkins loose. Close card.

9. Cut 5¼" x 6¾" rectangle from checkered card stock. Adhere rectangle onto inside middle section of card.

10. Cut 2½" x 3½" rectangle from white card stock.

11. Using black pen, write party information on rectangle.

12. Cut 6¼" x 4½" rectangle from black card stock. Adhere to checkered paper. See photograph on page 67.

13. Adhere white rectangle onto bottom right corner of black rectangle. Adhere small pumpkins to black rectangle as desired.

14. Thread ribbon through left slit, around back, and through right slit. Tie ribbon in bow on front of card.

Christmas Star

Materials & Tools

Card stock: cream; gold metallic; green

Christmas floral sticker

Craft knife

Pattern: Primitive Star (pg. 113)

Pens: gold metallic; red felt-tipped

Red satin ribbon: ¼"-wide (24")

Ruler

Instructions

Refer to General Instructions on pages 5–13.

1. Transfer Primitive Star Pattern onto metallic card stock. Repeat.

2. Cut out designs.

3. Cut 8½" x 5½" card from green card stock. Fold widthwise, meeting two ends in middle.

4. Using craft knife, cut ¾" slit in right side of one star and left side of remaining star.

5. Fold stars in half lengthwise. Adhere inside portion of each star to each inside flap, leaving outside flaps of star loose. Close card.

6. Cut 1½" x ¼" and 3¾" x ¼" strips from metallic paper. Cut strips in half widthwise.

7. Adhere two shorter strips ¼" down from top edge of card, meeting in middle. Repeat for remaining strips and bottom edge of card. See photograph.

8. Using gold pen, dot around stars on outside flaps.

9. Cut 3½" x 4½" rectangle from cream card stock. Place floral sticker on center top of rectangle.

10. Using red pen and ruler, create border around rectangle below sticker.

11. Cut mat ⅛" larger than rectangle all around from metallic card stock.

12. Center and adhere rectangle onto mat. Adhere mat onto inside section of card.

13. Thread ribbon through left slit, around back, and through right slit. Tie ribbon in bow on front of card.

Envelope Cards

Sometimes it is handy to have the card and envelope combined into one neat, little package. This combination is called an envelope card.

The photograph at right shows how the envelope card is creased on perforation lines. The envelope is sealed with a sticker, cut-out design, or die-cut, then unfolded to reveal the card, which is created directly onto the inside of the envelope.

It is also possible to cut the envelope from clear mylar (e.g. a page protector) so that the card sits separately inside and shows through the envelope. See page 74.

Note: When mailing square Envelope Cards, be certain to include extra postage stamps as needed.

This Envelope Card makes a great thank you card for bridal showers or weddings. Express your thoughts on a clear page protector, that is cut to fit over the color copy of the photograph. The top layer is held in place at the top with a floral sticker, which allows the recipient to lift the message for clearer view of the color-copied photograph beneath.

It's a Boy

Materials & Tools

Black felt-tipped pen

Card stock: cream; blue flecked with cream back; blue patterned; yellow; yellow patterned

Patterns: Baby Booties (pg. 117); Envelope #3 (pg. 116); Smaller Puffy Star (pg. 114); Smaller Puffy Star Mat (pg. 114)

Press-on letters for desired message: ¼"

Instructions

Refer to General Instructions on pages 5–13.

1. Enlarge Envelope #3 Pattern 46%. Transfer onto blue flecked card stock with solid back.

2. Transfer Baby Booties Pattern onto blue patterned card stock. Repeat with yellow card stock.

3. Transfer Smaller Puffy Star Mat Pattern onto yellow card stock.

4. Transfer Smaller Puffy Star Pattern onto blue patterned paper.

Continued on page 72.

Justin Ames
7 LBS. 6 OZS. 21"
March 25, 1997

Continued from page 71.

5. Cut out card and designs.

6. Cut 4" x 1⅜" rectangle from yellow card stock.

7. Cut mat ¹⁄₁₆" larger than rectangle all around from blue flecked card stock.

8. Center and adhere rectangle onto mat. Center and adhere mat onto front of envelope for mailing address.

9. Cut 5⅜" square from cream card stock.

10. Cut 5¼" square from yellow patterned card stock.

11. Center and adhere smaller square onto larger square.

12. Cut out yellow shoe laces from baby bootie. Adhere shoe laces over blue patterned baby booties.

13. Adhere baby booties onto square as desired. Center and adhere square onto inside of card.

14. Cut 1½" x ¾" rectangle from cream card stock.

15. Using black pen, write birth inforamtion on rectangle.

16. Cut mat ¹⁄₁₆" larger than rectangle from yellow card stock.

17. Cut second mat ½" larger than rectangle from blue flecked card stock.

18. Center and adhere rectangle onto yellow mat. Center and adhere smaller mat onto larger mat.

19. Place letters on baby bootie tops as desired.

20. Center and adhere smaller puffy star onto smaller puffy star mat.

21. Crease card on perforation lines.

22. Center and adhere puffy star where four corners of card meet to seal envelope closed.

Party Invitation

Materials & Tools

Black ink pad

Card stock: black; black/white checkered; green; red; white; yellow

Patterns: Envelope #3 (pg.116); Glass with Straws (pg. 116); Watermelon 1 (pg. 115); Watermelon 2 (pg. 115)

Rubber stamp: invitation

Ruler

Silver metallic pen

Instructions

Refer to General Instructions on pages 5–13.

1. Enlarge Envelope #3 Pattern 46%. Transfer pattern onto black cover stock.

2. Transfer Glass with Straws Pattern onto white card stock. Transfer area between perforated lines onto yellow card stock. Transfer straw onto red card stock.

3. Transfer Watermelon 1 Pattern onto green card stock. Repeat.

4. Transfer Watermelon 2 Pattern onto red card stock. Repeat. Repeat with black card stock. Repeat.

5. Cut out card and designs. Adhere red straws on top of straw. Using perforation as guide, adhere yellow lemonade onto glass. See photograph.

6. Cut 4" x 1⅝" rectangle from red card stock.

7. Center and adhere rectangle onto front of envelope for mailing address.

8. Using silver pen and ruler, create border around rectangle.

9. Cut 5⅞" x ½" rectangle from checkered card stock.

10. Cut mat ⅛" larger than rectangle from yellow card stock.

11. Cut second mat 1/16" larger than first mat all around from red card stock.

12. Center and adhere rectangle onto yellow mat. Center and adhere mat onto red mat.

13. Center and adhere mat ⅛" down onto top inside edge of card.

14. Using black ink pad and rubber stamp, stamp image onto glass. Note: If computer-generating invitation, print onto white card stock then transfer glass pattern around invitation.

15. Adhere glass onto left edge of card, extending straws into checkered border at top.

16. Trim black watermelon section 1/16" smaller than red watermelon section. Adhere sections together. Repeat for remaining watermelon sections.

17. Adhere red watermelon sections onto green watermelon sections, matching straight edges.

18. Adhere one watermelon onto bottom of card, overlapping glass.

19. Crease card on perforation lines.

20. Center and adhere remaining watermelon where four corners of card meet to seal envelope closed.

NAME _____
PLACE _____
DATE _____
TIME _____
PHONE _____

73

Thanks

Materials & Tools

Card stock: assorted colors; black; red; white

Clear page protector

Heart stickers: large (1); micro (4)

Patterns: Envelope #3
   (pg. 116); Hand
   (pg. 116); Thanks
   (pg. 118); Tiny Heart
   (pg. 109)

Pens: black felt-tipped;
   silver metallic

Instructions

Refer to General Instructions on pages 5–13.

1. Enlarge Envelope #3 Pattern 46%. Transfer pattern onto clear page protector.

2. Transfer Thanks Pattern onto assorted colored card stock. Repeat six times.

3. Transfer Hand Pattern onto white card stock.

4. Transfer Tiny Heart Pattern onto red card stock.

5. Cut out envelope and designs.

6. Crease envelope on perforation lines.

7. Cut 5⅜" square card from black card stock.

8. Using silver pen and ruler, create border around card. Write desired message on card.

9. Place one micro heart sticker on each corner of card.

10. Using black pen, write recipient's address on large heart sticker. Center and place large heart sticker on back side of black card.

11. Using silver pen, dot around heart.

12. Place card into envelope with address information, facing opposite of flaps.

13. Place assorted thanks into envelope as desired.

14. Adhere heart between thumb and forefinger of hand.

15. Center and adhere hand where four corners of envelope meet to seal envelope closed.

I've Moved

Materials & Tools

Card stock: assorted colors; black; red; white

Clear page protector

Craft knife

Double-sided tape

Patterns: Curved Arrow (pg. 116); Envelope #2 (pg. 119); Lollipop Alphabet (pg.125); Tiny Check Mark (pg. 115)

Pen: black felt-tipped; silver metallic; white felt-tipped

Ruler

Tiny heart stickers (4)

Instructions

Refer to General Instructions on pages 5–13.

1. Enlarge Envelope #2 Pattern 58%.

2. Transfer Envelope #2 Pattern onto clear page protector.

3. Transfer Curved Arrow Pattern onto white card stock.

4. Transfer Lollipop Alphabet for MOVED onto assorted colored card stocks, making certain to transfer each letter onto a different color of card stock. Note: Enlarge letters for MOVED as desired.

5. Transfer Tiny Check Mark Pattern onto red card stock.

6. Cut out envelope and designs. Using craft knife, cut slit in envelope.

Continued on page 76.

Continued from page 75.

7. Crease envelope on perforations lines.

8. Tape and seal side flaps.

9. Cut 3⅜" x 6¼" card from black cover stock.

10. Using silver pen and ruler, create border around card. Place one tiny heart sticker on each corner of card.

11. Cut 2¾" x ¾" rectangle from black cover stock.

12. Using white pen and ruler, create border around rectangle.

13. Write "IT OUT" on rectangle, leaving space for the check mark. Note: This can also be computer-generated with reverse type. Because the background is black, the paper will disappear when it is adhered to the card.

14. Adhere check mark onto left edge of rectangle, creating message ✓ IT OUT. Center and adhere rectangle onto card. See photograph.

15. Using silver pen, write desired message below rectangle on card. Write recipient's name and address horizontally on back of card.

16. Place card in envelope with address information, facing opposite of flap.

17. Drop letters into envelope as desired.

18. Insert envelope flap inside slit. Center and adhere arrow onto top of slit to seal envelope closed.

Faux Embossed Cards

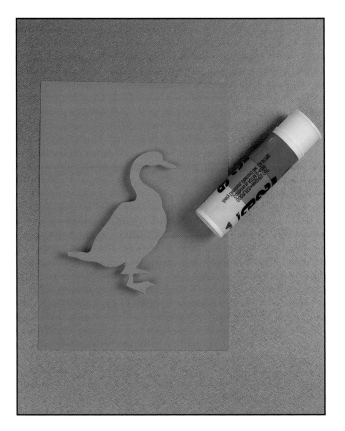

To emboss is to raise in relief, the surface of the card. Embossing adds a special touch of elegance to cards for all occasions.

Faux embossing is a shortcut that adds the beauty of embossing without the extra time.

Cut the embossed image from the same paper as the card on which it will sit. When the cut-out is fastened to the card, it gives the illusion of embossing because it is raised off the card surface. See photograph at left.

Beautiful pre-embossed card stock is also available in several different patterns. Create patterns from this paper, or use the paper as the card itself for an especially quick and easy elegance.

Embossing is particularly effective for wedding events, birth announcements, valentine and anniversary cards, or any time an elegant look is desired.

This Faux Embossed Card was created with pre-embossed card stock. Decorated with colored card stock and stickers, making greeting cards does not get any easier than this.

Gotta Have Heart

Materials & Tools

Card stock: cream;
  cream embossed;
  gold metallic; red

Cover stock: black

Gold metallic pen

Micro heart stickers (4)

Patterns: Heart #3A
  (pg. 118); Love
  (pg. 118)

Instructions

Refer to General Instructions on pages 5–13.

1. Transfer Heart #3A Pattern onto red card stock.

2. Transfer Love Pattern onto metallic card stock.

3. Cut out designs.

4. Cut 7" x 10" card from black cover stock. Fold in half widthwise.

5. Cut 4¼" x 6" rectangle from cream card stock.

6. Cut mat ⅟₁₆" larger than rectangle all around from metallic card stock.

7. Place micro heart stickers on top and bottom of rectangle. See photograph on facing page.

8. Center and adhere rectangle onto mat. Center and adhere mat onto inside of card.

9. Cut 3⅜" square from cream embossed card stock.

10. Cut mat ¹⁄₁₆" larger than square all around from metallic card stock.

11. Center and adhere heart onto square. Center and adhere square onto mat.

12. Center and adhere mat ½" down from top front of card.

13. Center and adhere Love below mat on front of card.

14. Using gold pen, dot around Love.

Love You

79

Materials & Tools

Black felt-tipped pen

Cover stock: craft; cream

Floral stickers: large;
  small

Pattern: Love (pg. 118)

Ruler

Instructions

Refer to General Instructions on pages 5–13.

1. Transfer Love Pattern onto cream card stock. Cut out design.

2. Cut 7" x 10" card from craft cover stock. Fold in half widthwise.

3. Cut 6" x 4" rectangle from cream card stock.

4. Cut fifteen ⅜" squares from cream card stock.

5. Adhere squares onto bottom of rectangle in checkerboard fashion. See photograph on page 79.

6. Center and adhere rectangle onto inside of card.

7. Using black pen and ruler, create border around rectangle.

8. Place small floral sticker on top inside edge of card, overlapping rectangle.

9. Cut 4⅞" x 3⅞" rectangle from cream card stock.

10. Center and adhere Love onto rectangle. Center and adhere rectangle onto front of card.

11. Using black pen and ruler, create border around rectangle.

12. Place large floral sticker on top edge front of card, slightly overlapping rectangle.

The faux embossed technique allows for other elements like checkered heart shown below to sit between the embossed element and the card.

Silly Goose

Materials & Tools

Black felt-tipped pen

Bow stickers: large; medium

Card stock: blue flecked; cream

Colored pencils

Cover stock: blue patterned with solid back

Pattern: Goose (pg. 119)

Instructions

Refer to General Instructions on pages 5–13.

1. Transfer Goose Pattern onto cream card stock.

2. Cut out design.

3. Cut 8" x 10¾" card from cover stock.

4. Fold cover stock in half widthwise.

5. Cut 4" x ⅜" rectangle from blue flecked card stock.

6. Center and adhere rectangle 1" down from inside top of card. Continued on page 82.

Continued from page 81.

7. Place medium bow on top edge of blue flecked rectangle, overlapping rectangle.

8. Cut 4¾" x 5¾" rectangle from cream card stock.

9. Using black pen and ruler, create border around rectangle. Create lines for desired message.

10. Center and adhere rectangle onto inside of card, below blue flecked rectangle.

11. Using colored pencils, lightly shade beak, feet and eye of goose. Place large bow sticker on goose's neck.

12. Cut 3⅜" x 4¼" rectangle from cream card stock.

13. Center and adhere goose onto cream rectangle.

14. Cut two 3¼" x ⅛" strips from blue flecked card stock. Cut two 4" x ⅛" strips from blue flecked card stock.

15. Adhere strips ⅛" in from edges of cream rectangle, overlapping corners creating border. See photograph on page 81.

16. Cut 2¼" x ⅛" strip from blue flecked card stock.

17. Center and adhere strip below goose inside of border.

18. Adhere rectangle to front of card 1" below top edge of card.

Season's Greetings

Materials & Tools

Card stock: cream; gold metallic

Cover stock: red

Craft punch: tiny star

Pattern: Tree Border (pg. 119)

Self-adhesive paper: gold metallic; red

Tiny heart stickers (4)

Instructions

Refer to General Instructions on pages 5–13.

1. Transfer Tree Border Pattern onto cream card stock.

2. Cut out design.

3. Cut 6½" x 9½" card from red cover stock. Fold in half widthwise.

4. Cut 3¾" x 5½" rectangle from cream card stock.

5. Cut mat ⅜" larger than rectangle all around from metallic card stock.

6. Cut two 3" x 1/16" and one 2½" x 1/16" strips from red card stock.

7. Center and adhere one 3" strip ¹⁄₁₆" from top edge of rectangle. Repeat with other 3" at bottom. Center and adhere remaining strip above bottom strip. Place star stickers on ends of top and bottom strips. See photograph.

8. Center and adhere rectangle onto mat. Center and adhere mat onto inside of card.

9. Cut 4½" x 6¼" rectangle from cream card stock.

10. Cut 3¾" x ¹⁄₁₆" and 4" x ¹⁄₁₆" strips from metallic card stock.

11. Center and adhere 4" strip ¼" up from bottom edge of rectangle. Center and adhere remaining strip ⅛" above bottom strip.

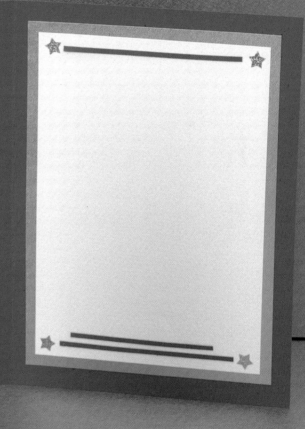

12. Center and adhere tree onto rectangle.

13. Using craft punch, punch out 12 stars from gold and red self-adhesive paper.

14. Place stars on tree and rectangle as desired.

Spiral Mobile Cards

A Spiral Mobile Card is one that arrives in a flat envelope and magically suspends from the ceiling for a unique and special three-dimensional greeting.

A spiral is used as the mechanism that holds each of the dangling elements. This type of mobile virtually eliminates the difficulties associated with balancing all of the elements and keeping the threads untangled. Plus, the mobile lies flat, making it easy to slide into an envelope and send through the mail.

To slide it into an envelope, simply lay the mobile flat on a sheet of paper, slide the paper into the envelope and remove the paper, leaving the spiral mobile inside.

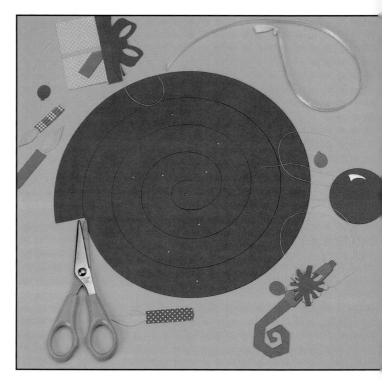

Envelopes are available in a variety of colors and 9" x 12" is the perfect size for holding larger Spiral Mobile Cards. An A-6 envelope is just the right size for the smaller spiral mobiles.

It is helpful to leave the thread long while fastening the shapes to the spiral. See photograph at left. When stickers are used to hold the thread, barely press down on each sticker while arranging the shapes. This allows the thread to be raised or lowered easily. When the arrangement is complete, press the stickers down firmly to hold the shapes in place and trim any excess thread.

Valentine
Sweetheart

Materials & Tools

Card stock: assorted red/white
  patterned; gray; red; tan;
  white

Craft knife

Hole punch: ¼"

Patterns: Cherub (pg. 121);
  Heart #1A (pg. 120);
  Primitive Hearts (pg. 107);
  Small Heart (pg. 119);
  Spiral (pg. 120); Tiny Heart
  (pg. 109);

Pens: black felt-tipped; silver
  metallic

Photograph

Poster board: black

Push pin

Red micro heart stickers

Red ink pad

Red satin ribbon: ¼"-wide
  (1 yd.)

White thread

Instructions

Refer to General Instructions on pages 5–13.

1. Enlarge Spiral Pattern 55%. Transfer pattern onto black poster board.

2. Transfer Heart #1A Pattern onto red card stock. Cut two. Note: This pattern will generate a heart frame and a heart.

3. Transfer Small Heart Pattern and Tiny Heart Pattern onto patterned card stocks. Cut two of each.

4. Transfer Cherub Pattern onto tan card stock. Cut two. Repeat with white card stock. Cut two.

5. Transfer Primitive Hearts Pattern onto assorted colored card stocks. Cut two.

6. Cut out spiral. Using craft knife, cut out inside heart from Heart #1A. Embellish cherub's wings with gray card stock on white wings.

7. Using black pen, draw eyes on cherubs.

8. Using ink pad, lightly ink finger tip and gently press finger on cherubs' cheeks.

9. Adhere black piece of card stock onto back of one heart frame. Using silver pen, write desired message on black section of heart frame.

10. Crop photograph to fit in heart frame. Adhere photograph behind heart frame with black heart as backing.

11. Using hole punch, punch hole in center of spiral. Cut 28" piece of ribbon. Insert ribbon through hole. Knot at one end to hold in place. Note: The ribbon will suspend the spiral from the ceiling.

12. Using push pin, pierce tiny holes in spiral to suspend designs.

13. Cut seven pieces of thread in desired lengths to hang designs from spiral.

14. Sandwich one end of thread vertically between each pair. Match and adhere pairs together.

15. Insert remaining end of thread through pierced holes. Repeat for all designs. Adhere thread onto spiral with micro heart stickers.

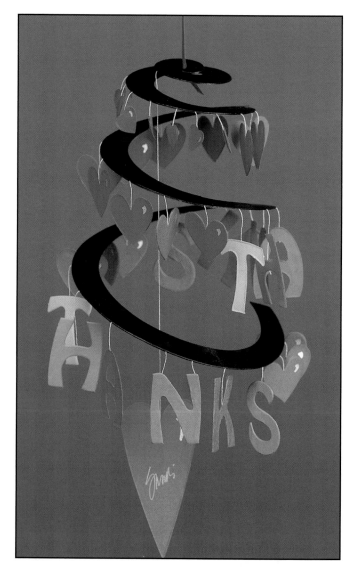

Above is another idea for a Spiral Mobile Card. Thread can be sandwiched between two matching designs which are then draped over the edges of the spiral. Each design is taped to top and an extra spiral is cut out to cover all of the tape.

Birthday Wishes

Materials & Tools

Black felt-tipped pen

Card stock: assorted colors; hot-pink; yellow

Craft punch: tiny balloon

Hole punch: ¼"

Patterns: Balloons (pg. 109); Candles (pg. 106); Gift Tag (pg. 120); Gift with Ribbon (pg. 120); Noisemaker (pg. 109); Numbers (pg.107); Spiral (pg. 120); Splash (pg. 109)

Poster board: blue

Push pins

White thread

Yellow satin ribbon: ⅛"-wide

Instructions

Refer to General Instructions on pages 5–13.

1. Enlarge Spiral Pattern 55%. Transfer pattern onto blue poster board.

2. Transfer Balloons Pattern onto assorted colored card stock. Cut two of each.

Continued on page 88.

Continued from page 87.

3. Transfer Candles Pattern onto assorted colored and yellow card stocks. Cut out seven pairs of candles.

4. Trim flame off of multicolored candles and adhere colored bases to yellow candles.

5. Transfer Gift Tag Pattern onto assorted colored card stock. Cut two.

6. Transfer Noisemaker Pattern onto hot-pink card stock. Cut two.

7. Transfer Numbers Pattern representing age of birthday onto assorted colored card stock. Cut two.

8. Transfer Gift with Ribbon Pattern onto assorted colored card stock. Cut four.

9. Transfer Splash Pattern onto assorted colored card stock. Cut two.

10. Using craft punch, punch out fifteen balloons from assorted colored card stock.

11. Cut out spiral. Embellish designs as desired.

12. Using black pen, write desired message on tag.

13. Using hole punch, punch hole in center of spiral. Cut 28" piece of ribbon. Insert ribbon through hole. Knot at one end to hold in place. Note: The ribbon will suspend the spiral from the ceiling.

14. Using push pins, pierce tiny holes in spiral to suspend designs.

15. Cut eight pieces of thread in desired lengths to hang designs from spiral.

16. Sandwich one end of thread vertically between each set of pairs. Match and adhere pairs together.

17. Insert remaining end of thread through pierced holes. Repeat for all designs. Adhere thread onto spiral with balloon punches.

New Arrival

Materials & Tools

Card stock: assorted colors; assorted patterns; blue; green; yellow

Hole punch: ¼"

Patterns: animals (pg. 121–122);9 Spiral (pg. 120); Tiny Star (pg. 122)

Pink heart stickers

Poster board: green

Push pin

White thread

Yellow satin ribbon: ¼"-wide (1 yd.)

Instructions

Refer to General Instructions on pages 5–13.

1. Enlarge Spiral Pattern 55%. Transfer pattern onto green poster board.

2. Transfer animal patterns onto assorted colored card stocks. Cut two of each.

3. Transfer Tiny Star Pattern onto yellow card stock. Cut four.

4. Cut out spiral. Embellish animals as desired.

5. Using hole punch, punch eyes in each animal. Adhere blue card stock behind eye openings of animals before matching and adhering pairs together.

6. Using hole punch, punch hole in center of spiral. Cut 28" piece of ribbon. Insert ribbon through hole. Knot at one end to hold in place. Note: The ribbon will suspend the spiral from the ceiling.

7. Using push pin, pierce tiny holes in spiral to suspend designs.

8. Cut eight pieces of thread in desired lengths to hang designs from spiral.

9. Sandwich one end of thread vertically between each set of pairs. Match and adhere pairs together.

10. Insert remaining end of thread through pierced holes. Repeat for all designs. Adhere thread onto spiral with heart stickers.

11. Place heart stickers back-to-back onto mobile threads as desired.

Mazel Tov

Materials & Tools

Card stock: gold metallic

Hole punch: ¼"

Patterns: Gift Tag (pg. 120); Spiral (pg. 120)

Poster board: blue

Push pin

Stickers: assorted Hanukkah stickers with symmetrical or mirror images; gold stars

White satin ribbon: ¼"-wide (1 yd.)

White thread

Instructions

Refer to General Instructions on pages 5–13.

1. Transfer Spiral Pattern onto blue poster board.

2. Transfer Gift Tag Pattern onto metallic card stock. Cut two.

3. Cut out spiral. Embellish gift tag with Hanukkah stickers.

4. Using hole punch, punch hole in center of spiral. Cut 28" piece of ribbon. Insert ribbon through hole. Knot at one end to hold in place. Note: The ribbon will suspend the spiral from the ceiling.

5. Sandwich one end of thread vertically between each set of stickers. Make certain stickers are symmetrical or are mirror images of each other. Match and adhere pairs together.

6. Using push pin, pierce tiny holes to suspend designs from spiral.

7. Insert remaining end of thread through pierced holes. Repeat for all designs. Adhere thread to spiral with gold star stickers.

Dangle Cards

Dangle Cards have one or more elements that are suspended so that they dangle and are visible through a window. The card can be positioned so that it reads vertically or horizontally.

Thread is sandwiched between two matching designs to create the hanging elements. A photograph can also be substituted for the design. It is important for the thread to be the same color as the background color of the card so that the shapes seem to magically suspend in midair.

Tape thread with design or photograph attached to the back of the card before adhering the cover to the card. See photograph below. Note: The cover is on the left and the card is on the right.

The card cover is free for a message or for designs themed to match the sentiments inside the card. The Dangle Card is a great vehicle for a word of encouragement ("Hang in There"); for a retirement message ("Time to Hang It Up"); or a card for anytime ("Just Hanging Around").

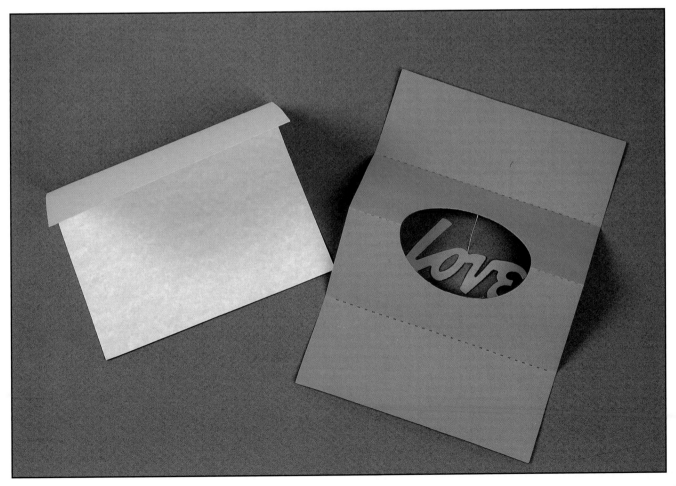

Just A Note

Materials & Tools

Black felt-tipped pen

Card stock: black/white polka-dot; black/white musical patterned; red; red/white polka-dot; white; yellow

Cover stock: black

Double-sided tape

Patterns: Accordion Card with Cut Out (pg. 123); Letters (pg. 125); Tiny Musical Note (pg. 122)

Press-on letters for Just A Note To Say: ¼"

Ruler

Transparent tape

Yellow thread

Instructions

Refer to General Instructions on pages 5–13.

1. Enlarge Accordion Card with Cut Out Pattern 63%. Transfer pattern onto musical patterned card stock.

2. Transfer Letters Pattern for H and I onto red/white polka-dot card stock. Repeat.

3. Transfer Tiny Musical Note onto black/white polka-dot card stock.

4. Cut out card and designs. Using craft knife, cut out window.

5. Crease card on perforation lines.

6. Cut 6¼" x 9¼" cover from cover stock. Fold in half widthwise.

7. Cut 6" x 9" lining from yellow card stock. Fold in half widthwise. Center and adhere lining to inside of cover, leaving black border all around.

8. Sandwich one end of thread vertically between each set of letters. Match and adhere letters together.

9. Tape thread to top inside opening of card so letters dangle in window. See photograph on facing page.

10. Cut 4¾" x 1½" rectangle from red card stock.

11. Using black pen and ruler, create border around inside edge of rectangle. Write desired message on rectangle.

12. Adhere rectangle onto bottom of card.

13. Cut 2" square from white card stock.

14. Using black pen and ruler, create border around inside edge of square. Adhere tiny musical note onto inside of square.

15. Cut 4½" x 3¼" rectangle from yellow card stock. Center and adhere white square onto rectangle.

16. Place letters on rectangle for Just A Note To Say.

17. Cut mat ¼" larger than rectangle all around from red card stock.

18. Adhere rectangle onto mat. Adhere mat onto front of cover.

19. Adhere one end of card ⅛" from top inside edge of cover. Repeat for remaining end of card and edge of cover.

A Thank You

Materials & Tools

Adhesive foam dots

Button: ¾" wooden heart

Card stock: assorted red patterned; denim

Cover stock: yellow/white checkered, two-sided

Craft knife

Craft punch: tiny heart

Double-sided tape

Patterns: Accordion Card with Cut Out (pg. 123); Heart #2 (pg. 122); Primitive Hearts (pg. 107)

Pens: black felt-tipped; silver metallic

Raffia scrap

Stickers: bow; tulip bouquet

Yellow thread

Instructions

Refer to General Instructions on pages 5–13.

1. Enlarge Accordion Card with Cut Out Pattern 63%. Transfer pattern onto denim card stock.

2. Transfer Heart #2 Pattern onto red patterned paper. Repeat.

3. Transfer Primitive Hearts Pattern onto red patterned card stock.

4. Cut out card and designs. Using craft knife, cut out window.

5. Crease card on perforation lines.

6. Cut 6½" x 9½" cover from cover stock. Fold in half widthwise.

Continued on page 94.

Continued from page 93.

7. Sandwich one end of thread vertically between small hearts. Match and adhere hearts together.

8. Tape thread to top inside opening of card so heart dangles in window. See photograph.

9. Using craft punch, punch out several hearts from red patterned paper. Adhere hearts around opening of card. See photograph.

10. Place bouquet sticker on bottom right of card. Place bow sticker over stems of bouquet.

11. Cut 2¼" x 1¼" rectangle from red patterned card stock.

12. Using black pen, write desired message on rectangle.

13. Cut mat ¼" larger than rectangle all around from yellow/white checkered card stock.

14. Adhere rectangle onto mat. Center and adhere mat onto top of card with foam dot.

15. Cut mat ¼" larger than primitive heart all around from red patterned card stock. Adhere primitive heart onto mat.

16. Cut 2½" x 6½" rectangle from denim card stock. Repeat. Adhere rectangles onto bottom front of card cover.

17. Center and adhere primitive heart at slight angle onto front of cover.

18. Thread raffia through button and tie in knot. Trim ends. Adhere button onto center of primitive heart.

19. Using silver pen, write desired message along right edge of primitive heart.

20. Adhere one end of card ⅛" from top inside edge of cover. Repeat for remaining end of card and edge of cover.

We're Engaged

Materials & Tools

Adhesive foam dots

Black felt-tipped pen

Card stock: cream; dk. tan; tan

Color copy of photograph

Cover stock: cream

Craft knife

Double-sided tape

Patterns: Accordion Card with Cut Out
 (pg. 123); Love (pg. 118)

Ruler

Stickers: assorted floral

Tan thread

Instructions

Refer to General Instructions on pages 5–13.

1. Enlarge Accordion Card with Cut Out Pattern 63%. Transfer pattern onto tan card stock.

2. Transfer Love Pattern onto cream card stock. Repeat.

3. Cut out card and designs. Using craft knife, cut out window.

4. Crease card on perforation lines.

5. Cut 9½" x 6½" cover from cover stock. Fold in half widthwise.

6. Sandwich one end of thread vertically between love pair. Match and adhere pair together.

Continued on page 96.

We're
Engaged

October 2, 1999

Continued from page 95.

7. Tape thread to top inside opening of card so love dangles in window. See photograph on page 95.

8. Place floral stickers around window of card as desired.

9. Cut 2¼" x ½" rectangle from cream card stock.

10. Using black pen and ruler, create border around rectangle. Write message on rectangle.

11. Center and adhere rectangle onto bottom of card.

12. Crop photograph to fit on top inside of card. Adhere photograph onto top of card.

13. Cut 9¼" x 6¼" mat from dk. tan card stock. Adhere mat onto inside of cover.

14. Cut 2¾" x 1¼" rectangle from cream card stock.

15. Using black pen and ruler, create border around rectangle. Write desired message on rectangle.

16. Cut 5" x 3¼" mat from dk. tan card stock. Center and adhere rectangle onto mat.

17. Cut second mat ¼" larger than first mat all around. Center and adhere mats together. Center and adhere mat onto front of cover.

18. Place floral sticker along top edge of mat, overlapping mat. Place foam dot on one floral sticker. Place floral sticker on bottom right edge of mat.

19. Adhere one end of card ⅛" from top inside edge of cover. Repeat for remaining end of card and edge of cover.

Working Too Hard

Materials & Tools

Adhesive foam dots

Blue thread

Card stock: black; cream; gold metallic; red; tan

Color-copied photograph and mirror image

Cover stock: blue

Double-sided tape

Patterns: Accordion Card with Cut Out (pg. 123); Clipboard (pg. 123); Pocket Watch (pg. 122)

Pens: gold metallic; white felt-tipped

Ruler

Instructions

Refer to General Instructions on pages 5–13.

1. Enlarge Accordion Card with Cut Out Pattern 63%. Transfer pattern onto tan card stock.

2. Transfer Clipboard Pattern onto onto red card stock. Repeat with black and gold card stocks.

3. Transfer Pocket Watch Pattern onto black card stock. Repeat with cream, gold, and red card stocks.

4. Cut out card and designs. Using craft knife, cut out window. Embellish clipboard and pocket watch as desired.

5. Crease card on perforation lines.

6. Assemble pocket watch and adhere onto left side of card. See photograph below.

7. Cut 9½" x 6½" cover from cover stock. Fold in half widthwise.

13. Tape thread to top inside opening of card so photograph dangles in window. See photograph below.

14. Adhere clipboard onto front of cover as desired.

8. Cut ½" x 4" rectangle from black card stock.

9. Using white pen and ruler, create border around rectangle. Write desired message on rectangle.

10. Adhere rectangle onto right edge card.

11. Crop mirror-image photograph as desired for dangling element.

12. Sandwich one end of thread vertically between photographs. Match and adhere pair together.

15. Cut 3" x ¾" strip from black card stock. Using white pen and ruler, create border around strip. Write desired message.

16. Cut mat ⅛" larger than strip all around from red card stock.

17. Center and adhere rectangle onto mat. Center and adhere mat onto bottom front of cover.

18. Adhere one end of card ⅛" from top inside edge of cover. Repeat for remaining end of card and edge of cover.

Diorama Cards

Diorama Cards provide a quick and easy way to send a three-dimensional message. The card lies flat for mailing, but converts easily to 3-D in the hands of the recipient. See photograph at right for Diorama Card after it is cut out.

Creasing on the perforation lines, and sliding the inside "card tab" through the slit, creates a simple but effective three-dimensional card with lots of room for themed decoration.

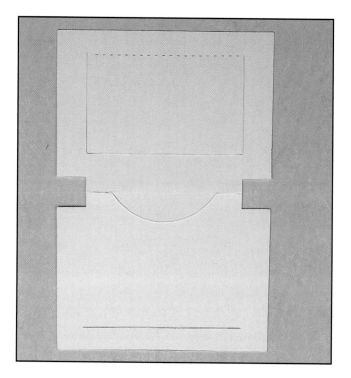

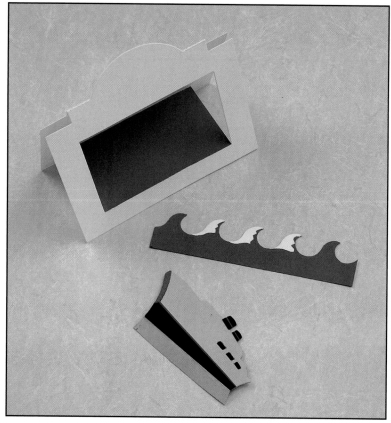

Whether the designs are attached to the card tab by a fold, or inserted through slits cut in the card tab, assembly is easy.

Create Diorama Cards for any occasion by matching the design elements to the theme of the card.

Happy Happy Birthday

Materials & Tools

Adhesive foam dots

Card stock: assorted colors; assorted patterns; black; red; white; yellow

Cover stock: black

Craft knife

Double-sided tape

Patterns: Balloon (pg. 124); Candles (pg. 106); Diorama Arch Card (pg. 124)

Pens: silver metallic; white

Ruler

Sticker strips: assorted colors

Instructions

Refer to General Instructions on pages 5–13.

1. Enlarge Diorama Arch Card Pattern 60%. Transfer pattern onto black cover stock.

2. Transfer Balloon Pattern onto assorted card stock. Repeat.

3. Transfer Candles Pattern onto assorted colored and yellow card stocks. Cut out candles.

Continued on page 100.

Continued from page 99.

4. Trim flame off of assorted colored candles and adhere onto yellow candles.

5. Cut out card. Using craft knife cut slits in card.

6. Crease card on perforation lines.

7. Cut 6¼" x 4¾" rectangle from red card stock.

8. Adhere red rectangle onto back inside of card.

9. Cut 3½" x 1¼" rectangle from black card stock.

10. Using white pen and ruler, create border around rectangle. Write desired message on rectangle.

11. Cut mat ¼" larger than black rectangle all around from white card stock.

12. Adhere rectangle onto mat. Center and adhere mat onto inside back of card.

13. Using silver pen and ruler, create border around front of card.

14. Cut strip sticker into confetti. Place confetti on front of card.

15. Place foam dot on back of one balloon. Place balloons on right top front of card, overlapping foam-dotted balloon on top.

16. Using silver pen, draw highlights on balloons. Draw balloon strings.

17. Tape candles together in groups of twos and threes. Fold candle ends under ¼". Cut three slits in card tab for candles.

18. Slip folded ends of candle groups through slits. Tape ends to back of tab, allowing candles to stand up.

19. Slip tab into card slit to assemble card.

This basic Diorama Card can be decorated for any occasion by altering the theme of the designs.

100

Jesse

Materials & Tools

Blue felt-tipped marker

Card stock: blue; blue/white polka-dot;
  dk. blue; yellow/white checkered

Cover stock: cream

Craft knife

Double-sided tape

Patterns: Baby Bootie (pg. 123);
  Diorama Stage Card (pg. 124)

Press-on letters for name: ¼"

Ruler

Instructions

Refer to General Instructions on pages 5–13.

1. Enlarge Diorama Stage Card Pattern 64%. Transfer pattern onto cream cover stock.

2. Transfer front section of Diorama Stage Card Pattern onto blue card stock for card border.

3. Transfer Baby Bootie Pattern onto fold of blue/white polka-dot card stock. Note: Cutting bootie on the fold creates a tab for attaching it to card. Repeat with cream card stock.

4. Transfer back of Diorama Stage Card Pattern onto yellow/white checkered card stock for lining.

5. Cut out card and designs. Embellish bootie as desired. Using craft knife, cut slits.

6. Adhere checkered lining onto inside back of card.

7. Using craft knife and ruler, cut out ½"-wide border from blue card front. See photograph.

8. Adhere blue border of card onto front of card.

9. Adhere a piece of dk. blue card stock onto back of bootie opening. Adhere laces onto bootie.

10. Tape bootie's tab onto card tab, allowing bootie to stand up.

11. Place letters on top arch of card for name.

12. Using blue marker, write birth information above card front opening.

13. Slip tab into slit to assemble card.

Bon Voyage

Materials & Tools

Adhesive foam dots

Card stock: black; blue; gold; dk. gray; gray; orange; red

Cover stock: white

Craft punch: sun

Double-sided tape

Hole punch: 1/16"

Patterns: Diorama Stage Card (pg. 124); Ocean Liner (pg. 122); Waves (pg. 124)

Press-on letters for desired message: 1/4"

Instructions

Refer to General Instructions on pages 5–13.

1. Enlarge Diorama Stage Card Pattern 64%. Transfer onto white cover stock.

2. Transfer back section of Diorama Stage Card Pattern onto gold card stock.

3. Transfer Waves Pattern onto blue card stock.

4. Transfer Ocean Liner Pattern onto fold of gray card stock. Note: Cutting ocean liner on the fold, creates a tab for attaching it to card. Repeat on black; dk. gray; and red card stocks for embellishing ocean liner. Cut out designs.

5. Crease card on perforation lines. Embellish ocean liner as desired. Using craft knife, cut slits.

6. Adhere back section of card onto inside of card. Adhere a piece of blue card stock onto tab of card.

7. Cut three caps for waves from white cover stock. Adhere caps to desired waves. Adhere waves 1/8" from bottom of card.

8. Cut 1/16" border from black card stock to go around top curve of card. Adhere border around top curve.

9. Using hole punch, punch three holes at end of each border.

10. Adhere a piece of black card stock behind holes.

11. Tape ocean liner's tab onto card tab, allowing ocean liner to stand up.

12. Using craft punch, punch out sun from yellow card stock. Repeat on orange card stock. Adhere suns together, allowing orange sun to show through yellow sun.

13. Place sun onto top center of card below black border with foam dot.

14. Place letters on card for desired message.

15. Slip tab into slit to assemble card.

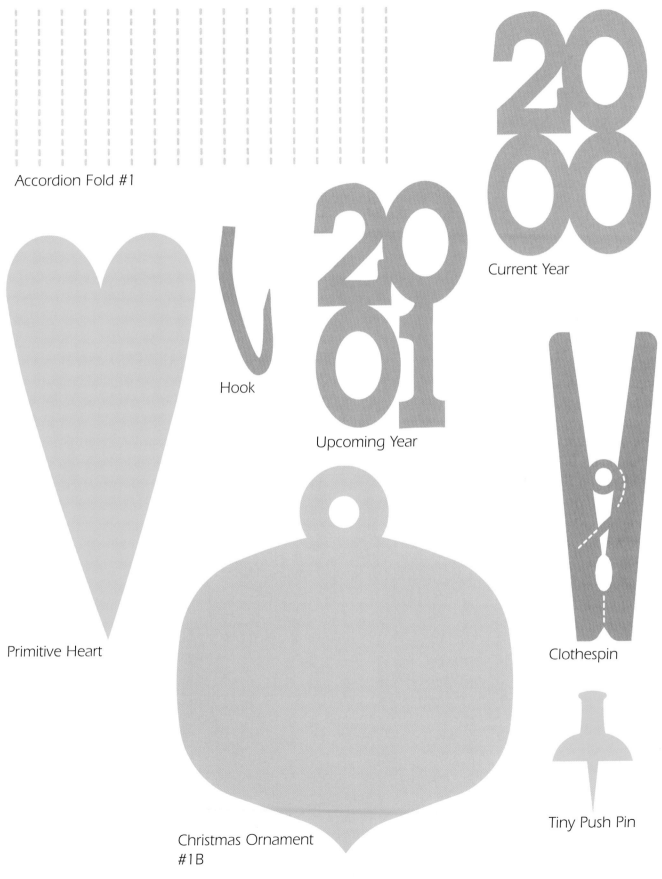

Accordion Fold #1

Current Year

Hook

Upcoming Year

Clothespin

Primitive Heart

Christmas Ornament
#1B

Tiny Push Pin

103

Accordion Card

Tiny Christmas Light

Primitive Star

Holly Leaves

Christmas Ornament #2A

Country Christmas Tree

Large Accordion Card

Accordion Fold #2

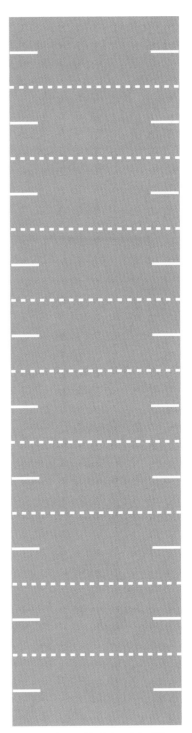

Accordion Fold with Slits

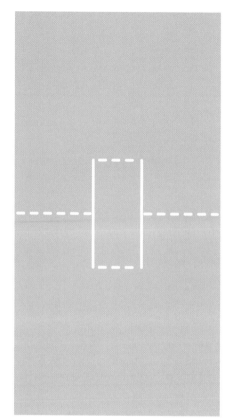

Pop-Up #1

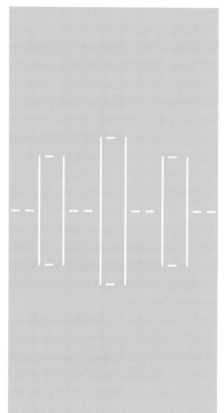

Pop-Up #3

Candles

Tiny Pumpkin

Arrow

Ghost #2

0123456789

Numbers

Primitive Hearts

Small Primitive Star

Tiny Button

Carrot

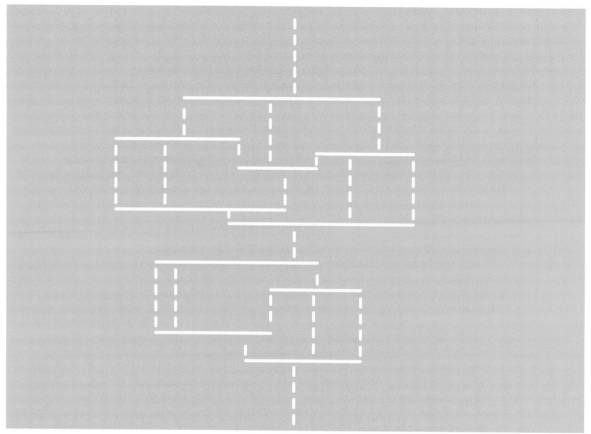

Multiple Pop-Up #1

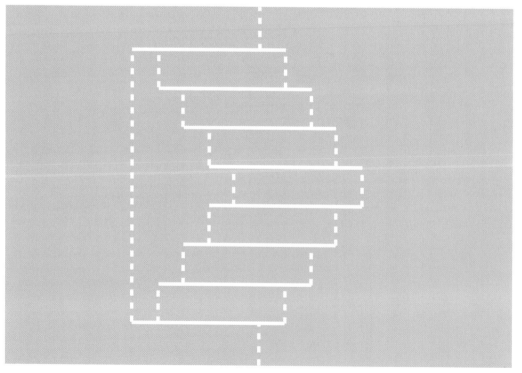

Multiple Pop-Up #2

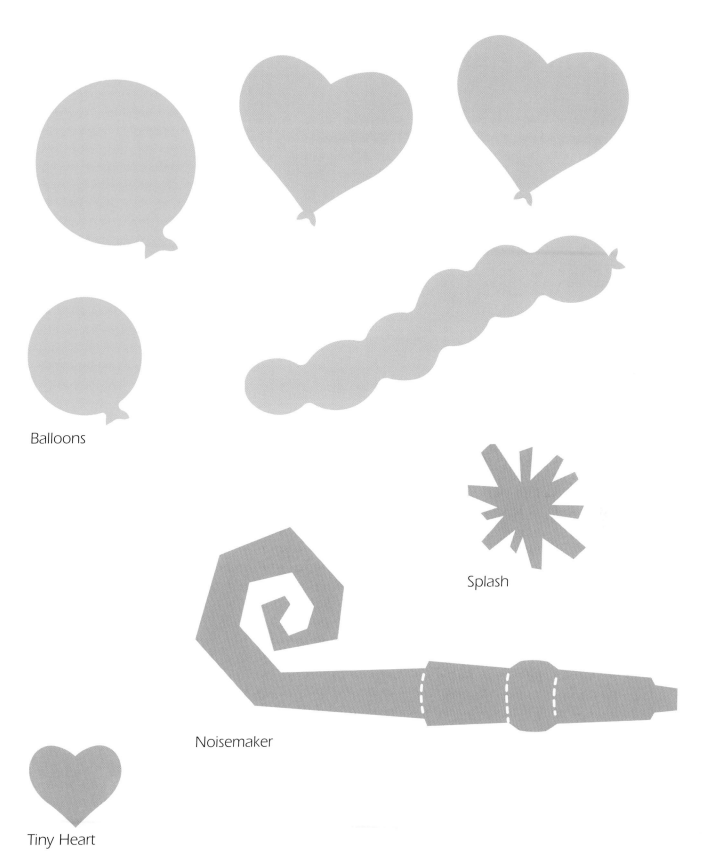

Balloons

Splash

Noisemaker

Tiny Heart

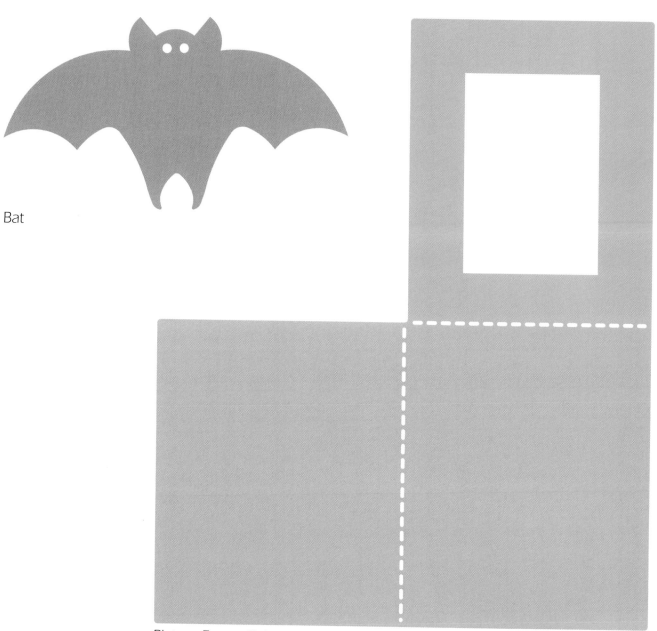

Bat

Picture Frame Fold Up Card

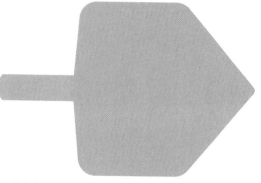

Dreidel

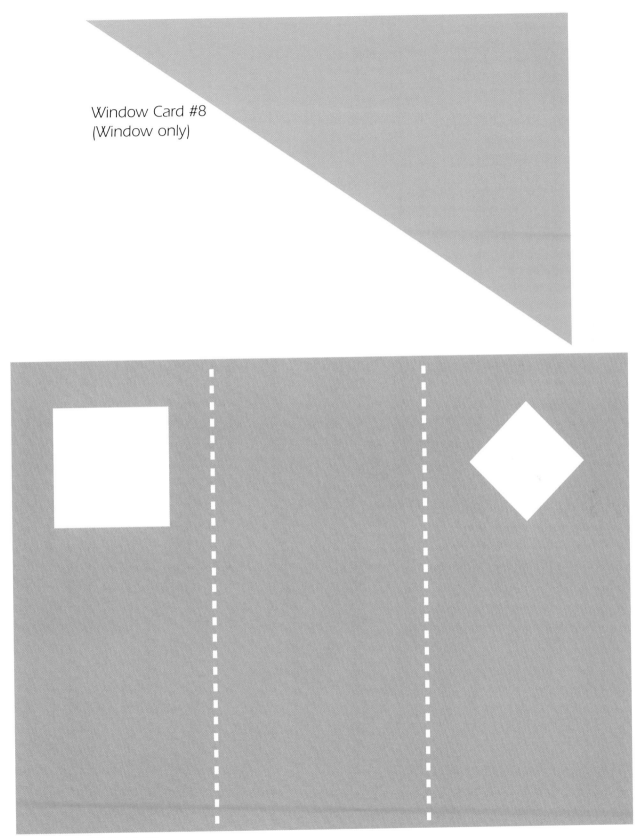

Window Card #8
(Window only)

Geometric Tri-Fold #2

111

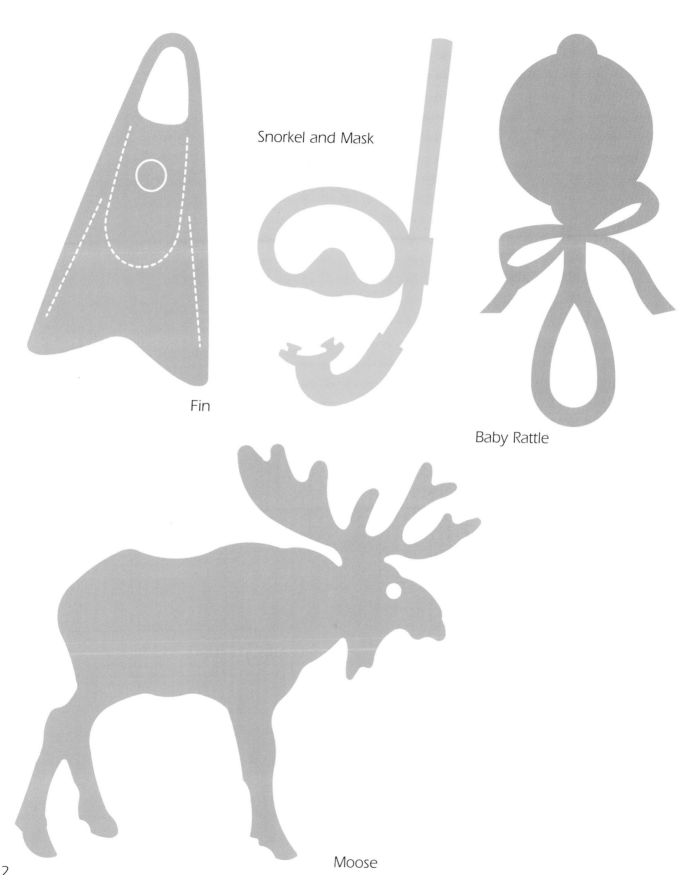

Snorkel and Mask

Fin

Baby Rattle

Moose

Balloons

Fishing Pole

Tiny Fish

Primitive Star

Pumpkin

Window Card #5

Smaller Puffy Star

Smaller Puffy Star Mat

Overlapping Card A

Overlapping Card B

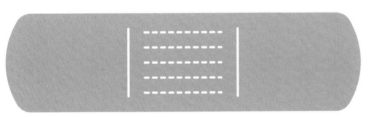

Bandage

Watermelon 1

Tiny Check Mark

Watermelon 2

Envelope #3

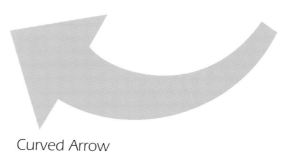

Curved Arrow

Glass with Straws

Hand

116

Baby Booties

Larger Puffy Star

Larger Puffy Star Mat (optional)

Thanks

Love

Heart #3A

Envelope #2A

Small Heart

Goose

Tree Border

119

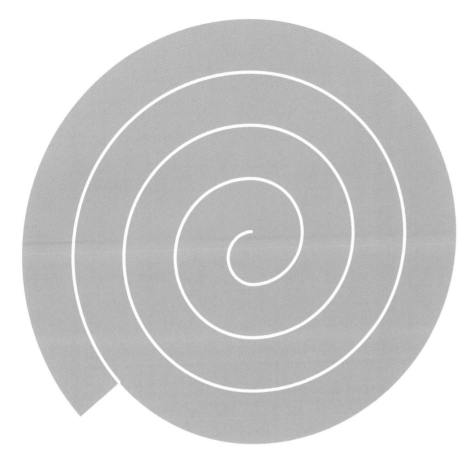

Spiral

Gift Tag

Gift with Ribbon

Heart #1A

120

Fish #2

Cherub

Lamb Toy

Duck Toy

Pig Toy

Chick Toy

Tiny Star

Tiny Musical Note

Rabbit #4

Heart #2

Ocean Liner

Pocket Watch

122

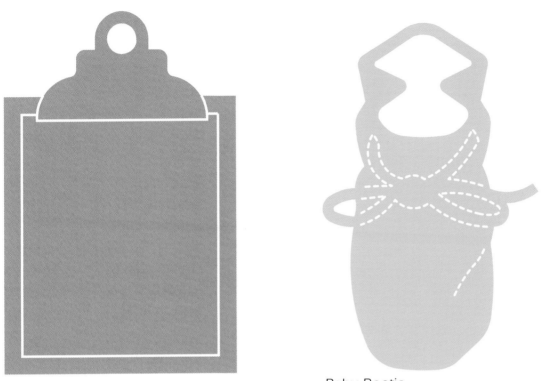

Clipboard

Baby Bootie

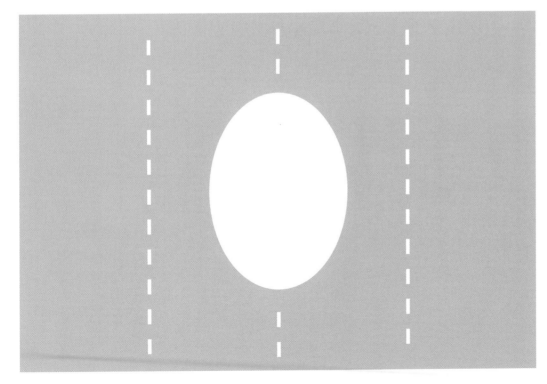

Accordion Card with Cut Out

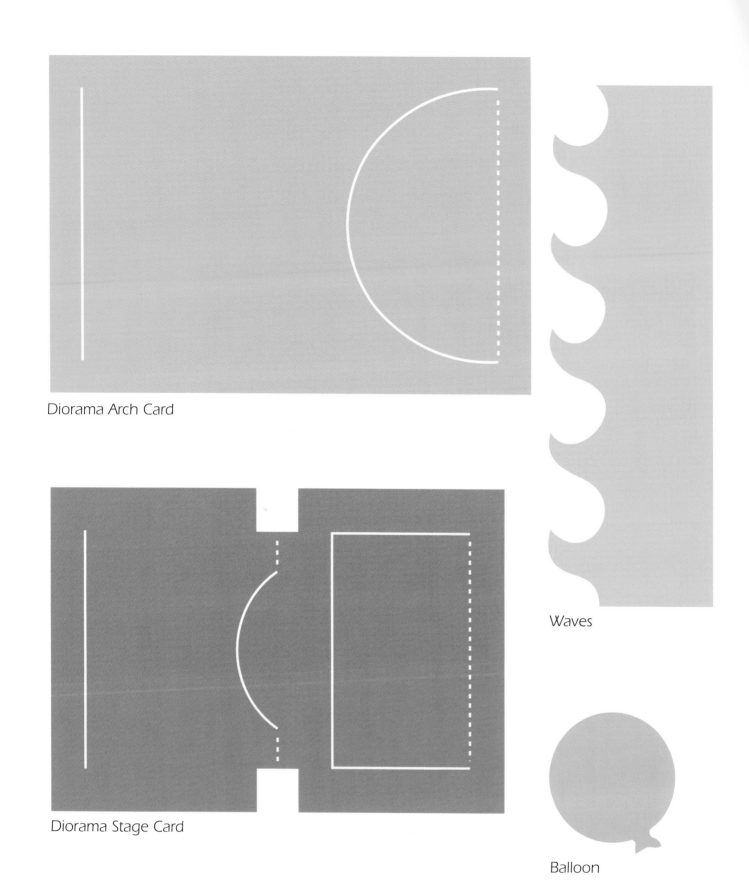

Diorama Arch Card

Diorama Stage Card

Waves

Balloon

ABCDEFGHI
JKLMNOPQ
RSTUVWXYZ
abcdefghi
jklmnopqrs
tuvwxyz;'?(!)

Lollipop Alphabet

Ellison® Dies

Name	Stock No.
Cards, Envelopes and Folds:	
Accordion Card	A102
Accordion Card With Cut Out	A103
Accordion Fold #1	A100
Accordion Fold #2	A101
Diorama Arch Card	C196
Diorama Stage Card	C197
Envelope #2A	E5002
Envelope #3	E5003
Geometric Tri-Fold #2	C192
Multiple Pop-Up #1	P800
Multiple Pop-Up #2	P799
Picture Frame Fold Up Card	P518
Pop-Up #1	P811
Pop-Up #3	P813
Window Card #5	C201
Window Card #8	C204
Decorative Dies:	
Arrow	H318
Baby Bootie	B106
Baby Booties	B107
Baby Rattle	B097
Balloons	B130, B132
Bandage	B142
Bat	B154
Candles	C156
Carrot	F790

Name	Stock No.
Cherub	C415
Chick Toy	C441
Christmas Ornament #1B	C474
Christmas Ornament #2A	C475
Clipboard	C520
Clothespin	C538
Country Christmas Tree	C488
Curved Arrow	A801
Dreidel	D670
Duck Toy	D891
Fin	S992
Fish #2	F482
Fishing Pole	F491
Ghost #2	G451
Gift Tag	T145
Gift with Ribbon	G454
Glass with Straws	G509
Goose	G660
Hand	C446
Heart #1A	H315
Heart #2	H312
Heart #3A	H313
Holly Leaves	H770
Lamb Toy	L101
Large Puffy Star	S814
Lollipop Alphabet (lower case)	2"
(upper case)	4"
Love	W923
Moose	M703

Name	Stock No.
Noisemaker (Party Noisemaker #2)	P176
Ocean Liner	D120
Pig Toy	P533
Pocket Watch	W156
Primitive Heart	H316
Primitive Hearts	H316
Primitive Star	S817
Pumpkin	P900
Puffy Star Mat	S809
Rabbit #4	R102
Small Primitive Star	S818
Small Puffy Star	S814
Snorkel and Mask	S457
Spiral	S760
Splash	P176
Thanks	W910
Tiny Balloons	B131
Tiny Button	B982
Tiny Check Mark	C405
Tiny Christmas Light	C481
Tiny Fish	F483
Tiny Heart	H310, H320
Tiny Musical Note	M902
Tiny Pumpkin	B770TU
Tiny Push Pin	P941
Tiny Star	S812
Tree Border	B770TR
Watermelon1	W160
Watermelon 2	W160
Waves	D56013

Metric Conversion Chart

mm-millimetres   cm-centimetres
inches to millimetres and centimetres

inches	mm	cm	inches	cm	inches	cm
⅛	3	0.3	9	22.9	30	76.2
¼	6	0.6	10	25.4	31	78.7
⅜	10	1.0	11	27.9	32	81.3
½	13	1.3	12	30.5	33	83.8
⅝	16	1.6	13	33.0	34	86.4
¾	19	1.9	14	35.6	35	88.9
⅞	22	2.2	15	38.1	36	91.4
1	25	2.5	16	40.6	37	94.0
1¼	32	3.2	17	43.2	38	96.5
1½	38	3.8	18	45.7	39	99.1
1¾	44	4.4	19	48.3	40	101.6
2	51	5.1	20	50.8	41	104.1
2½	64	6.4	21	53.3	42	106.7
3	76	7.6	22	55.9	43	109.2
3½	89	8.9	23	58.4	44	111.8
4	102	10.2	24	61.0	45	114.3
4½	114	11.4	25	63.5	46	116.8
5	127	12.7	26	66.0	47	119.4
6	152	15.2	27	68.6	48	121.9
7	178	17.8	28	71.1	49	124.5
8	203	20.3	29	73.7	50	127.0

yards to metres

yards	metres	yards	metres	yards	metres	yards	metres	yards	metres
⅛	0.11	2⅛	1.94	4⅛	3.77	6⅛	5.60	8⅛	7.43
¼	0.23	2¼	2.06	4¼	3.89	6¼	5.72	8¼	7.54
⅜	0.34	2⅜	2.17	4⅜	4.00	6⅜	5.83	8⅜	7.66
½	0.46	2½	2.29	4½	4.11	6½	5.94	8½	7.77
⅝	0.57	2⅝	2.40	4⅝	4.23	6⅝	6.06	8⅝	7.89
¾	0.69	2¾	2.51	4¾	4.34	6¾	6.17	8¾	8.00
⅞	0.80	2⅞	2.63	4⅞	4.46	6⅞	6.29	8⅞	8.12
1	0.91	3	2.74	5	4.57	7	6.40	9	8.23
1⅛	1.03	3⅛	2.86	5⅛	4.69	7⅛	6.52	9⅛	8.34
1¼	1.14	3¼	2.97	5¼	4.80	7¼	6.63	9¼	8.46
1⅜	1.26	3⅜	3.09	5⅜	4.91	7⅜	6.74	9⅜	8.57
1½	1.37	3½	3.20	5½	5.03	7½	6.86	9½	8.69
1⅝	1.49	3⅝	3.31	5⅝	5.14	7⅝	6.97	9⅝	8.80
1¾	1.60	3¾	3.43	5¾	5.26	7¾	7.09	9¾	8.92
1⅞	1.71	3⅞	3.54	5⅞	5.37	7⅞	7.20	9⅞	9.03
2	1.83	4	3.66	6	5.49	8	7.32	10	9.14

Index